D1029733

DISCARDED

ALSO BY MAURIZIO VIROLI

Niccolò's Smile

REPUBLICANISM

REPUBLICANISM

Maurizio Viroli

Translated from the Italian by Antony Shugaar

 *Hill and Wang*

A division of Farrar, Straus and Giroux

New York

Hill and Wang
A division of Farrar, Straus and Giroux
19 Union Square West, New York 10003

Copyright © 1999 by Gius. Laterza & Figli Spa, Roma-Bari
Translation copyright © 2002 by Farrar, Straus and Giroux
All rights reserved
Distributed in Canada by Douglas & McIntyre Ltd.
Printed in the United States of America
Originally published in 1999 by Gius. Laterza & Figli Spa, Roma-Bari,
as *Repubblicanesimo*
Published in the United States by Hill and Wang
First American edition, 2002

Library of Congress Cataloging-in-Publication Data
Viroli, Maurizio.
   [Repubblicanesimo. English]
   Republicanism / Maurizio Viroli.— 1st ed.
      p.   cm.
   Includes bibliographical references and index.
   ISBN 0-8090-8077-X (hc : alk. paper)
      1. Representative government and representation—History. 2. Republi-
canism—History. I. Title.

JF1051 .V57 2002
321.8'6—dc21   2001039556

Designed by Jonathan D. Lippincott

www.fsgbooks.com

10 9 8 7 6 5 4 3 2 1

To Michael Walzer

Contents

Foreword

I WROTE THIS book with the hope that in the first instance it might help to strengthen the civic consciousness of my country's political leaders and citizens. Recent political events indicate, however, that the prevailing mood in Italy is to sustain principles that are the opposite of what I consider civic ideals. With their vote in the elections of May 13, 2001, a majority of Italians indicated that they consider the liberty to pursue one's self-interest more important than respect for the rule of law. They also showed they are not concerned that the man they elected prime minister, Silvio Berlusconi, owns three major television stations, newspapers, and publishing houses, has immense wealth, and rules a party of men and women who are totally loyal to him—and therefore concentrates in his hands a personal power that no democratic leader before him has ever enjoyed. They also appear to think it normal for the public good to be subordinated to factional interests. And since that election, many Italians and others have also indicated, in their response to what happened in

Genoa in the summer of 2001 during the meeting of the Group of Eight, that they favor a strong state over a state that protects civil rights.

There are two Italys in fact, as recent sociological studies have shown. One is composed of people who are concerned only with their families and their own personal success, the other of people who have a strong civic awareness and are actively engaged in commitments to their community, to the needy, to the environment, even at the cost of sacrificing their own interests. As in any country, the boundaries between these two groups are not rigid: civic Italians may become uncivic; uncivic Italians may discover the dignity of a life informed by ideals of democratic citizenship. And of course there are also significant overlaps, inasmuch as one and the same person can be a fervent opponent of certain social rights and yet be active in the community. The problem is that uncivic Italy is far stronger than civic Italy, and this is true for many other countries as well.

If we consider the two facts together—the weakening of civic spirit and the rise to power of a leader like Berlusconi—we must conclude that European and American political commentators have every reason to worry. Italy could become a democratic society with a regime that has given unchallenged power to a man or a group and that has come to power without needing to violate democratic and liberal norms. By using money, charisma, and the persuasive power of media under his control, an ambitious man might be able to gain the popular consensus he wants without breaking the rules of a constitutional democracy.

This decline in civic consciousness is a trend that affects other Western democracies too, not least the United States.

The consequences differ in different countries, but the weakening of civic spirit opens a path to power everywhere for the wealthy or for demagogues (or a combination of the two). For this reason, I hope that my reflections on the most effective ways to strengthen civic spirit in democratic societies, composed from an Italian perspective, may be useful for American citizens and political leaders.

M.V.
August 2001

REPUBLICANISM

A New Interpretation of Republicanism

THE FIRST REPUBLICS without slaves were created in Italy at the end of the Middle Ages. Within the city walls of Florence, Venice, Genoa, Pisa, Lucca, Siena, and other Italian towns, there were no princes and no kings but citizens living together under common laws and statutes, even if citizenship in its fullest sense was the privilege of only a minority among them. And within these walls, in public councils and in the studies of jurists, historians, and political theorists, was created modern republican thought, a distinctive body of political theory committed to sustaining the principle of liberty and to explaining the political and legal means to attain and preserve it.

To be the first does not mean to be the best. But political theorists tend to forget pieces of wisdom that earlier thinkers had already set forth and studied. I believe this is the case with a number of the political ideas that belong to republicanism.

REPUBLICANISM

Unlike a natural science, political science proceeds not by inventing new theories to replace old ones but by rediscovering and refining forgotten ideas and themes; and sometimes the work of rediscovery helps actual political practice. It is with this in mind that I am proposing this consideration of republicanism, written from an Italian perspective for English-speaking readers.

Republicanism in its classical version, which I identify with Niccolò Machiavelli, is not a theory of participatory democracy, as some theorists claim, having in mind more recent sources.[1] It is, rather, a theory of political liberty that considers citizens' participation in sovereign deliberation necessary to the defense of liberty only when it remains within well-defined boundaries. Maintaining that sovereign deliberations—deliberations that concern the whole body of citizens—must be entrusted to the citizens themselves, republican theorists derived their principle of self-government from the Roman law that "what affects all must be decided by all."[2] The idea was that self-interest would recommend to citizens that they deliberate for the common good, since those who participated were all equally affected.

If sovereign deliberations are entrusted to a large body rather than a small one, it is more likely that the council or legislature will have the political strength to carry out the common good against factional interests. Here Machiavelli's wisdom offers us a valuable insight about the much-contested and unclear conception of the common good. For him the common good is neither the good (or interest) of all citizens nor a transcendent or higher good that all citizens are supposed to identify and then aspire to, detaching themselves from their special interests and parochial loyalties. For Machiavelli the common good is the good of citizens who do not want to be oppressed and have no ambition to dominate.[3] He equates the desire not to be dominated with the desire to be free, and he argues that republics are better equipped to pursue the common good than political units governed by princes.[4]

Theorists of the early Italian republics all supported the doctrine that the form of government that best promotes the common good is a combination of the three classical forms of good government—the rule of one (monarchy), of the few (aristocracy), and of the many (republican or popular government)—and was best exemplified by the Republic of Venice. They all defended mixed government on the grounds that it provided different social groups an adequate place in the republic's institutional life and ensured the right balance among different aspects of sovereign power (legislative, deliberative, and executive). Some theorists, like Francesco Guicciardini, maintained that the making of new laws or the correction of old ones should be entrusted to restricted, carefully chosen groups because they believed that ordinary citizens were incompetent for the task.[5] Others, like Machiavelli, maintained that citizens in large deliberative bodies ought to be able to propose new laws, not just approve or reject laws framed by the smaller bodies. But even the most convinced advocates of the virtue of large bodies stressed that these should not deliberate on all political matters and should never be entrusted with absolute powers.

These republican theorists understood the principle of representation, and the early republics' legislative bodies were based on it. Fourteenth- and fifteenth-century jurists discussed it with reference both to councils as a whole and to individual citizens serving on them. They stipulated that a council as a whole represent the whole city or the entire people, not merely a part of the people. As for the individual citizen, he was expected to attend to the interests of the city and not the interests of his family or of the faction or group that elected him. This meant, as I say, that republicanism was a theory not of direct participatory democracy but of representative self-government within constitutional boundaries.

Another conventional view that I intend to challenge in this study is that republicanism is an alternative to liberalism. The truth is that liberal political theory has inherited a number of political ideas from classical republicanism, beginning with the fundamental principle that sovereign power must always be limited by constitutional and legal norms. It has also inherited the principle of political individualism—more precisely, the idea that the main goal of political society is to protect the individual, his or her life, liberty, and property. Liberal theorists rightly defend this principle against communitarians, but classical republicans had already stressed that the state is there to protect individuals' life, liberty, and property.

The principle of the separation of powers was also familiar to early-modern republican theorists, and early-modern republics practiced it, at least partially, as long as they survived. These theorists knew that to concentrate judicial and legislative power in the same body was dangerous for the maintenance of individual liberty. It was with this in mind that Machiavelli praised the Republic of Lucca and that Donato Giannotti, a few years later, criticized the Florentine Republic of 1494–1512.[6] So although liberal theorists have greatly refined our ideas about the functions of sovereign power, neither the principle nor the practice of dividing these functions was a liberal invention.

A distinctive feature of liberalism that is completely absent from early-modern Italian republicanism, however, is the theory of the natural (or inalienable, or innate) rights of man. This doctrine is fundamental, but it suffers from the obvious theoretical weakness that rights are (more or less) respected only when sustained by laws and customs. Rights are thus historical, not natural, and when they are not sustained by laws and customs, they are not rights but moral claims—noble, decent, and reasonable, but only claims. It is for this reason that Machiavelli, wiser than later theorists, had no use for the idea of natural rights and spoke only of liberty as a good that individuals may enjoy if they have good political and military institutions, if they possess a sufficient degree of civic virtue, and if they have the good luck not to live too close to powerful and aggressive neighbors.

These points suggest that we should reconsider the conventional geography of political theory. Republicanism is all too often seen as a province of democratic theory bordering on the large empire of liberalism. But it is historically more correct to regard both liberal and democratic political theory as provinces of republicanism, based in its classical form on the two principles of the rule of law and of popular sovereignty.[7] Liberal and democratic theory each emphasizes one of these two and diminishes the relevance of the other: the former emphasizes the rule of law, the latter popular sovereignty. There are, of course, many examples of liberals who praise popular sovereignty, advocating liberal democracy as opposed to liberal aristocracy or liberal monarchy. And many democrats praise the rule of law and advocate constitutional democracies as opposed to populistic or demotic ones based on the absolute power of an assembly (and of demagogues). Still, it is fair to describe liberalism as a tradition of political thought in which constitutional and legal limits on sovereign power are considered the safest bastions of liberty, and democratic theory as one that celebrates the virtues of popular sovereignty. If this is correct, we are compelled to conclude that they are both parts of a larger and richer republican theory. We must even consider the disquieting idea that the transformation of classical republicanism into the two traditions of liberalism and democratic theory should be not praised but lamented. Perhaps, to put it differently, splitting Machiavelli's legacy between Locke and Montesquieu, on the one hand, and Rousseau, on the other, has been an intellectual loss, not a gain.

The intellectual and political loss becomes more apparent when we compare the classical republican ideal of political liberty with the liberal and democratic ideals predominant in our political culture today (the first more than the second). Classical republican writers maintained that to be free means not to be dominated—that is, not to be dependent on the arbitrary will of other individuals. The source of this interpretation of political liberty was the principle of Roman law that defines the status of a free person as not being subject to the arbitrary will of another person—in contrast to a slave, who is dependent on another person's will. As the individual is free when he or she has legal and political rights, so a people or a city is free insofar as it lives under its own laws. The implication is that if the people of a city or a nation receive their laws from a king, they are not free but serfs; they are not at liberty but in servitude; their position is analogous to that of a slave before his master. Monarchy, which for the Romans meant monarchy in its absolute form, was equated with domination.

Classical republican theorists also stressed that the constraint that fair laws impose on an individual's choices is not a restriction of liberty but an essential element of political liberty itself. They also believed that restrictions imposed by the law on the actions of rulers as well as of ordinary citizens are the only valid shield against coercion on the part of any person or persons. Machiavelli forcefully expressed this belief in his *Discourses on Livy* (I.29), when he wrote that if there is even one citizen whom the magistrates fear and who has the power to break the law, then the entire city cannot be said to be free. It can be said to be free only when its laws and constitutional orders effectively restrain the arrogance of nobles and the licentiousness of the people.

Rousseau puts very clearly the difference between obedience and servitude when he writes: "A free people obeys, but it does not serve, it has leaders but no masters; it obeys the laws, but it obeys only the laws, and it is due to the strength of the laws that it is not forced to obey men." He identifies freedom with obedience to laws that impose the same constraints on everyone; conversely, he equates unfreedom with privilege—when some individuals have the power to exempt themselves from the constraints imposed on others:

> The Citizen desires the law and that the law should be observed. Every individual knows well that if exceptions to the law are allowed they will not work in his favor.

> Thus everyone has reason to fear the practice of making special exceptions, and this very fear is an indication that he loves the law. But with the ruling classes it is quite different: their social condition is based on privilege, and they seek such privileges everywhere. If they want to have laws it is not in order to obey them, but to be the judges.[8]

Here we see how the republican ideal of political liberty differs from the liberal ideal. According to the former, we are free so long as we are not dependent; according to the latter, we are free so long as we are free from interference. A person can be free from interference but still be dependent, like a slave of a good master who lets him do what he likes but remains his master. Conversely, a person can be independent but not free from interference, like a free citizen who is subject only to legitimate laws but must fulfill a number of civic duties and obligations. The central point for classical republican theorists is that dependence is a more painful violation of liberty than interference.

The democratic ideal of political liberty, understood as a condition in which citizens have autonomy and are governed by laws that reflect their will, is in fact a radical version of the republican ideal of political liberty as absence of domination. If to be free means that one is not subject to the arbitrary will of a man or group, as republican theorists claim, we enjoy complete political liberty when we are dependent only on our own will—that is, when we live in a self-governing polity that permits us to approve or reject the rules governing the life of the collectivity.

Democratic liberty is a type of positive liberty that expresses itself in direct participation in sovereign deliberations. Republican liberty is a type of negative liberty that individuals enjoy when they are free from domination, when they are not subject to the arbitrary will of an individual or group. From these different interpretations of liberty follow different interpretations of the significance of political participation. Democratic theorists consider political participation as something democratic institutions ought to promote in every possible way; republican theorists think of it as a means to protect liberty and to select the most virtuous and best-qualified citizens for positions of leadership, thus encouraging a political culture that is hostile to domination. Political engagement educates citizens who are not prepared to serve the whims of powerful individuals but who are ready, willing, and able to serve the common good. It tries to inspire a mentality that is hostile to both servility and arrogance and that considers liberty neither as a good we possess regardless of what we do or don't do nor as a condition we enjoy when we sit in sovereign legislative bodies, but as a good we have to earn and deserve.

This idea of political liberty, with all its moral and aesthetic implications, is more congenial to and better serves the political goals of a republic than the liberal conception (and the liberal ethos), because it is in fact impossible to be free from domination and from the obligations and interferences imposed by law, as a few examples illustrate. To emancipate women from the domination of men, a republic must impose laws that interfere with men's freedom of choice. To emancipate workers from the arbitrary power of employers, a republic must impose laws that restrict the employers' freedom of choice. To permit many people to enjoy the social rights that are indispensable to attaining and practicing citizenship, a republic must impose fair taxes and collect the needed resources. These examples clearly show that a conception of political liberty that rejects domination but is not hostile to obligations serves well the main purpose of a republic. Hostility to domination and to interference (possibly more to interference than to domination) does not help the republic to be what it should be, namely, an association of persons in which no one is allowed to dominate and no one is forced to serve.

This classical republican interpretation of political liberty has a wider emancipatory meaning than any liberal one. Liberal liberty aims to protect individuals only from interferences, from actions interfering with their freedom of choice; republican liberty aims to emancipate them also from conditions of dependence. What worries a liberal is having anyone's freedom of action dominated or controlled; a republican worries about this but worries even more about the dispiritedness that affects men and women who live dependent lives. Civic culture in democratic societies is suffocated by the persistence of arbitrary powers and practices of domination. Republicanism can help to remedy the consequent weakness of our democracies today.

Republicanism is a theory not only of political liberty but also of the passions that political liberty needs. The political wisdom that republican theorists have repeated with little variation over the centuries is that liberty can survive only if citizens possess that special passion called civic virtue. As I try to explain in this book, civic virtue is not a martial, heroic, and austere virtue but a civilized, ordinary, and tolerant one of citizens of commercial republics. It combines severity and playfulness, integrity and transgression, gravity and lightness. This is what Machiavelli taught us with his writings and his life.

Theorists of the early Italian republics equated civic virtue with the love of country, and they described true love of the republic as a passion that translated into acts of service and acts of care. It is precisely this meaning of love of country that has been almost entirely lost in contemporary democratic theory. The sad consequence is that our intellectual life offers us either patriots and nationalists who do not like political liberty or liberals and democrats who do not like republican patriotism.

Once, though, the republic was considered to be a political ordering and a way of life, a culture. Machiavelli speaks, for instance, of "affection for the free way of life," and other writers of his time defined the republic as "a particular way of life of the city." This means that republican patriotism is first of all a political passion based on the experience of citizenship, not on shared pre-political elements derived from being born in the same territory, belonging to the same race, speaking the same language, worshipping the same gods, having the same customs. The political experience of republican liberty, or the memory or hope thereof, makes the spaces, buildings, and streets of the city meaningful. Republican theorists knew well that the kind of commonality generated by inhabiting the same city or nation, speaking the same language, and worshipping the same gods is hardly sufficient to generate patriotism in the hearts of citizens: a true fatherland, they claimed, can only be a free republic. They also claimed that love of country is not a natural feeling but a passion that needs to be stimulated through laws or, more precisely, through good government and the participation of the citizens in public life.

As Margaret Canovan has correctly written, my position can be described as a defense of a "rooted republican patriotism," which is the opposite of Jürgen Habermas's constitutional patriotism. Habermas sees patriotism as consisting of a loyalty to the universalist political principles of liberty and democracy embodied in the constitution of the postwar Federal Republic of Germany. My patriotism is explicitly particularistic, because it describes love of country as the citizens' passionate love of their republic's institutions and way of life, and it remains particular, even though it can easily translate into active and passionate solidarity with other peoples. However particularistic, it is "free of illiberal characteristics because it is a 'patriotism without nationalism,'" and it is critical inasmuch as it is "dedicated to making sure that one's polity lives up to its highest traditions and ideals." However, according to Canovan, my version of patriotism "trades on a caricature of nationalism as a bigoted and racist commitment to ethnic and cultural homogeneity" and does not take into account that while "there is plenty of evidence of racist versions of nationalism (as of chauvinistic versions of patriotism), there is also a long-standing association between some nationalisms and liberal democracy."[9]

Of course, the ideal of nation has also been used to sustain projects of liberty and social justice. The best examples can be found in the works of nineteenth-century republicans: Carlo Pisacane, to mention one example, wrote that the principle of nationality that had excited the most generous souls in 1848 was an ideal of liberty. Like Giuseppe Mazzini, Pisacane interpreted this as the opposite of nationalism. Nationality for him meant the free expression of the collective will of a people, a common interest, full and absolute liberty, and no privileged classes, groups, or dynasties. Love of country, he explained, can only grow on the soil of liberty, and liberty alone can turn citizens into supporters of the republic. Under the yoke of princes and monarchs the generous passions of patriotism are bound to degenerate.[10]

Still, if by nationalism we mean what the late-eighteenth-century founders of the language of nationalism meant and most nationalist theorists mean today, it seems clear that republican patriots and nationalists disagreed on the central issue of what a true *patria* is. Theorists began their efforts to build the new language of nationalism precisely by attacking the republican principle that only a self-governing republic is a true nation. They also disagreed on what true love of country is or should be. Republican patriots considered love of country an artificial passion to be instilled and constantly reinforced by political means; nationalists thought of it as a natural feeling to be protected from cultural contamination and cultural assimilation. The *patria* of the republicans is a moral and political institution; the nation of the nationalists is a natural creation. Republics originated in the outstanding virtue and wisdom of legendary founders or from the citizens' free agreement; nations from God himself.

Even a modern theorist like Amy Gutmann, who accepts the view that republican patriotism is "anti-nationalistic, and defined in contrast to nationalism," considers my position "not without dangers due to its over-evaluation of the republic relative to the individuals that constitute it." Intrinsic to republican patriotism, she argues, "is the idea that the subordination of the self to society is obligatory (for the sake of realizing 'common liberty')." Moreover, republican patriotism is prone to claims of exclusivity that conflict with the openness of democratic education, as reflected in my assertion that "'the cause of liberty does not need cosmopolitans; it simply needs patriots.'"[11]

George Kateb, too, points to the anti-individualistic content of republican patriotism, which, he writes, is "a form of group identity and affiliation." Even if republican patriotism is a "patriotism of liberty," it still proclaims the necessity of incorporating the moral principle of liberty within one's own country. "I am put in mind," Kateb writes, "of the Catholic view that the immaterial and spiritual God cannot be loved without either the incarnation or such devices as Mariolatry, or statues and paintings of saints, or imposing and gorgeous houses of worship." The nefarious consequence of republican patriotism is that it teaches the patriot that he "must unhesitantly prefer inflicting injustice to suffering it." History, after all, shows that patriotism, with a few exceptions, has always served unjust or stupid or irrational causes. The thoughts and feelings "that called modern constitutional freedom into being and sustained it were not patriotic, but universalistic."[12]

I could respond that people motivated by republican patriotism have greatly contributed to the birth of modern constitutional democracies. As I try to show here, republican patriotism inspired England's "Commonwealth Men," Americans who fought for independence, French revolutionaries, and the many partisans of the Italian Resistenza who believed that to fight against Mussolini and Hitler was a patriotic duty. I have no problem acknowledging that in each of these cases patriotism had a particular connotation, in the sense that the patriots loved the liberty of their own people. But is their love of liberty of lesser moral dignity than love of liberty understood as a universal moral principle? Republican patriotism is capable of crossing national boundaries. It is stronger than cultural and religious differences. A person who loves the common liberty of his or her own people also loves and respects the liberty of other peoples and commits himself or herself to defending it. I am not claiming that the patriot's love of liberty is more intense than the universalist's, only that it is equal to it morally. Just as the God who lives in the particular has the same worth as the spiritual God, to use Kateb's analogy, so the liberty of a people has the same moral worth as individual liberty understood as a universal principle without reference to a given country or history.

With this difference—and this is my response to Gutmann's argument: it is in fact utterly impossible to live as a free individual in an unfree republic and among an unfree people. This means that when the advocates of republican patriotism encourage citizens to consider common liberty the highest good, they are indicating the safest means to protect individual liberty, not a way to enslave the individual to the state. And when they assert that the liberty one enjoys in one's own country is richer than the liberty one may find in a foreign country, they are sustaining an idea of individual liberty. If we taught young people this kind of republican patriotism, I believe we would have a good chance of educating them to be good citizens.

The task of educating good citizens and good political leaders cannot be fulfilled unless we rediscover yet another piece of classical republican wisdom: namely, that political theory is a department not of philosophy, or law, or science but of rhetoric. Contemporary political theorists compose their books and write their essays with the aim of producing reasonable arguments designed to win the readers' rational agreement. Machiavelli and other republican theorists conceived and practiced political theory as a *rhetorical* pursuit. This means that they composed their works with the purpose of persuading their readers to accept or reject particular political ideas by winning their rational assent but also by moving their passions. They intended to empower reason with eloquence, *ratio* with *oratio*, and for this reason they used examples, metaphors, narratives, exhortations, and all the other weapons of classical rhetoric.

At the risk of being called an unrepentant nostalgic, I believe that the old way was better than the new one and that the evolution of political theory away from rhetoric toward analytic philosophy, which began with Hobbes and attained its perfection with John Rawls, has been in stylistic terms a decay, not a progress. Leaving aside the obvious (but not irrelevant) consideration that works like Machiavelli's *The Prince* or *The Discourses on Livy* have a literary beauty that contemporary works in political theory do not even aim to achieve, it is evident that the idea of political theory as a philosophical enterprise conflicts with the realities of political life today and in particular with democratic deliberation as we know it. Unlike contemporary political theorists who presume that legislative deliberations offer the give-and-take of reasoned argument in a public forum that aims at justifying a mutually binding decision, classical republicans believed that what in fact occurs in deliberative councils is the give-and-take of partisan arguments couched rhetorically. These arguments may include reasoned claims, but they are fundamentally aimed at moving the listeners' passions. Real republics, therefore, are republics not of reason, as Philip Pettit has written, but of eloquence.[13] Contemporary democratic theorists respond to this by saying they hope that eloquence can be replaced by principled and reasoned public arguments. The more intelligent among republican theorists respond by urging citizens and political leaders to learn how to master eloquence.

Which choice is politically wiser I leave the reader to decide. But the main reason I believe we should retrieve the rhetorical style of political theorizing that enjoyed unchallenged hegemony through the seventeenth century is that it is more effective. Very rarely, nowadays or ever, do citizens endorse or reject political values by judging them from a detached, rational point of view. Rather, they form their ideas on the basis of feelings and emotions. If we learn the old rhetorical style, designed to win the reason's assent and to move the passions, we have a better chance of persuading our leaders and our fellow citizens to accept and to put into practice the political principles congenial to the life of a democratic republic. Isn't that, after all, the main task of political theory?

The Story Begins in Italy

EVEN THOUGH MODERN REPUBLICANISM origi-
nated in Italy, the revival of republicanism in political
thought at the end of the twentieth century revolved
around British and American universities. Even now, it has
only been paid lip service in Italy, where the chief concern of
political theorists seems to be an ongoing commentary on various versions of liberalism or rehashed discussions about the
distinction between true liberalism and false liberalism.[1]

The rebirth of republicanism ought rightly, however, to
interest us all, and certainly Italians. It was precisely the free
republics of Italy, between the fourteenth century and the early
sixteenth century, that witnessed the birth of that "classical
republicanism" which served as the fountainhead for the many
republican theories and political movements that flourished in
the next centuries in the Netherlands, England, France, and
the United States. We may no longer remember this, but

republican political thought was one of the most significant contributions that Italy ever offered to modernity.[2] Moreover, the republic, or perhaps we should say the republics, of Italy left indelible marks on the country's culture, language, and the appearance of its cities and countryside—not only the better-known republics, such as Florence, Venice, Siena, Genoa, and Lucca, but also the "forgotten republics."[3]

To rediscover the history of Italy's republics and their tradition of republican political thought is an opportunity to revive one of the richest aspects of modern history. Reconsidering and remembering this history do not necessarily mean that we shall find consolation or edification. Historians have rightly emphasized that the Italian republics of the Middle Ages were hardly models of liberty and justice, as they proclaimed themselves to be. They were communities dominated, some to a lesser and some to a greater degree, by narrow oligarchies of the wealthiest, most powerful families fiercely defending their own privileges, tyrannizing the peasants in the surrounding countryside, and not thinking in national terms.

Republican theorists were fully aware of these problems. If Florence were to be endowed with a true militia that might free it from the blight of mercenary troops, Machiavelli believed, the Florentine Republic would have to become more just in city and in countryside.[4] Donato Giannotti observed of Florence under Pier Soderini that "the city was held under the power of a very few," and in such circumstances there cannot be a "broad governance, which is to say free and peaceful; instead, a narrow governance that is tyrannical and violent." And Francesco Guicciardini, in his *Dialogue on the Government of Florence*, maintained that the insignia of Florentine liberty were to be taken "as camouflage and justification" rather than as symbols of the city's political reality. In Lucca the highest city magistrates proclaimed proudly in 1542 that the republic there "is the most popular government in Italy, and never deliberates save in the presence of a hundred or so councillors," but, as one scholar has put it, "everyone knew that the problem was that authority had been concentrated not in a few citizens but in a few families."[5]

None of this, however, belies the fact that the free republics were experiments in government that ultimately intended to allow a broad portion of the populace—at least broad for those times—to take part in the government and the sovereign power. Those republics were representative governments based on councils, which in their entirety represented the people or the city—and this was especially true of the great councils, or the largest assemblies. The task of selecting personnel for the government itself was entrusted to electoral commissions, which had to ascertain that all candidates met the standards for holding public office. If we consider the right to be elected to public office a distinctive element of the republican experience, this right was, in Florence, for instance, quite broadly exercised; but the actual participation of citizens in the decision-making processes was very different. The roughly three thousand public offices that were filled anew each year in Florence were occupied by only a tiny fraction of the number of citizens who theoretically had a right to hold them. Still, the tendency of the most powerful families to monopolize government offices was offset by the power of the legislative councils, notably councils of the sixteen districts into which the city was divided—the *gonfaloni*. The citizens who sat on the legislative councils considered themselves, and were considered, governmental representatives according to the modern understanding of the concept of representation. Matteo Palmieri, in *Vita Civile* (1435–1440), wrote: "Every good citizen placed in a magistracy in which he represents any principal component of the city considers himself before all else . . . a representative of the universal interests of the entire city." Florentines, like the citizens of other republics, were eager (out of ambition, interest, or civic pride) to participate in the legislative councils and to be elected to government office, as was shown by the general enthusiasm with which they greeted the establishment of the Consiglio Grande, or great council, in 1494.[6]

The guiding principle of republican governments was the city. "There was no lord to be served, because the citizenry alone stood at the center of the interests of the ruler," as Mario Ascheri wrote about Siena in the time of the Nove, or Nine (1287–1355). Siena's oligarchic government during that period of some seventy years saw two or three thousand citizens (out of a population of forty to fifty thousand) occupy the governing offices of the city.[7] In the Italian republics, such participation was regulated by written rules; the statutes had as their principal goal to make it as difficult as possible for any single family or man to form a regime or monopolize the public powers. The politicians of Siena selected to hold its highest offices—to be one of the Nine—served for just two months, and they were required by law to wait twenty months before they could once again do so. Because selection took place by a drawing, no one was certain to be chosen as one of the Nine. Lastly, strict rules forbade election to the Nine if a relative, family member, or business partner or associate held office in another civic institution.

What is even today a vague democratic utopia—the possibility of calling those in power to account for the way they perform their duties—was common practice in the Italian republics. At the end of their terms in office, in fact, the magistrates were investigated by special commissions with real and substantial powers of review. In Siena there also existed a Maggior Sindaco, or great syndic, whose task it was to ensure that public deliberations were conducted in full respect of the procedures defined by the statutes. Nor was Siena exceptional, since in Genoa the principle was long established that the actions of public functionaries had to comply with specific criteria defined by law. To ensure that the rules were followed, there was "a specific mechanism of review exercised by a magistracy established for this particular purpose," that is, the syndicate. The jurists and politicians of Genoa considered the possibility of enjoining magistrates to respect the rules, under the threat of sanctions, a fundamental element of their republican liberty.[8]

Recent historical research confirms, in broad outlines, the assessment made by Simonde de Sismondi in his *History of the Italian Republics*, written in the early nineteenth century. The Italian republics, wrote Sismondi, were a basic experience of modern liberty because, in contrast with Athens and Rome, they did not base their economic and social life on slavery and they admirably reconciled individual liberty with the pursuit of wealth and with intellectual and artistic life. Indeed, they created and diffused throughout Europe "the science of governing men for their own good, for the development of their industrial, intellectual, and moral faculties, for the increase of their happiness." With the science of good government arose a "republican spirit that was seen to ferment in all the cities, and which gave all those cities constitutions of such wisdom, magistrates of such zeal, and citizens animated by such great patriotism and capable of such great deeds."[9] His view was later confirmed by Carlo Cattaneo in an essay titled "The City Considered as the Ideal Principle of Italian History" (1858). Cattaneo reiterates that the Italian republics, especially Florence, could claim unquestionable credit for "having spread all the way down to the lowermost plebeians a sense of civil dignity and rights," and in this they had outdone even ancient Athens, "whose noble citizenry nonetheless rested on a substratum of slavery."[10]

The "sense of civil dignity and rights" that the free republics instilled in their citizens by summoning them to participate in public life has been kept alive over the centuries and has become one of the strong points of Italy's fragile democracy. This fact was brought to general attention a few years ago by Robert Putnam, who proved, with documents and maps, that democracy worked best in those parts of Italy that had once enjoyed republican self-government.[11]

How and why did this centuries-old way of life remain active through the ages? This is a mystery that resists our understanding. But it is not hard to see why citizens who are summoned to take part in public life should develop a mentality different from those who, generation after generation, live as subjects of a monarch, prince, or pope. And the difference lies in the fact that the former learn the art of living as citizens whereas the latter learn the art of living as subjects.

Aside from handing down a sense of civic dignity, early-modern Italian republics also bequeathed to us several major theoretical principles, such as the very concept of the independent republic. It was Italian jurists and philosophers of the fourteenth century who developed the classical concept of liberty when they worked out the principle that a city can call itself free if it does not depend on the will of the emperor, if it receives from the emperor no statutes or laws, and if it requires of him no approval of any sort. Cities that live in liberty (*"que vivunt in propria libertate"*) enjoy self-government (*"proprio regimine"*). According to the renowned phrase of Bartolus of Sassoferrato, these cities recognize no higher power (*"civitas quem superiorem non recognoscit"*), and therefore their people are a free people (*"populus liber"*).

Another theoretical contribution is the justification of the democratic constitution by virtue of the principle, taken from Roman law, of *quod omnes tangit*, which states, "That which concerns the many must be decided by the entire sovereign body of the citizens, acting in respect for law and in accordance with procedures established by statutes." If public deliberations concerning the entire city are entrusted to councils representing the entire citizenry, the republican theorists explained, it is more likely that sovereign decisions will affirm the common good, rather than the personal interests of rulers or a political faction or a social group, and will therefore protect the citizens from domination.[12]

Theorists of later centuries developed a theory of the republic as a form of mixed government that blended the positive aspects of three right forms of rule: the rule of one (monarchy), the rule of the few (aristocracy), and the rule of the many (popular or democratic government). The richest workshop in which to test the theory of mixed government was the Republic of Venice. Aside from Venice's own historians and statesmen, sixteenth-century political writers who considered mixed government included Niccolò Machiavelli, Francesco Guicciardini, and Donato Giannotti; these men elevated modern republicanism to a high level of theoretical development or, as some have described it, to its "classic" phase. In their view the theory of mixed government first of all fulfilled the political requirement of ensuring that a republic guaranteed the three essential functions of government: rapid implementation of sovereign deliberations, coordination and oversight of foreign policy, and other activities of government (in Venice this was ascribed to a doge or gonfalonier for life); an adequate pool of political skills (a Senate comprising the most experienced and respected citizens); and a reliable barrier against any attempt to establish tyranny or impose factional power (a Great, or Extended, Council with the power to approve laws and to choose the magistrates entrusted with actual rule). The theory of mixed government, moreover, also guaranteed that all the components of the city had an adequate role in public institutions. The office of doge or gonfalonier, along with the most important positions of the republic, could satisfy the appetites of the most ambitious citizens; the Senate, or a more restricted council such as that of the Pregàdi in Venice, would satisfy the ambitions of the "middle" citizens; while the Great Council met the requirements of citizens with no special desire for honor or glory but desirous of ensuring that the republic passed no unjust laws or summoned evil or corrupt men to public office.

Machiavelli, Guicciardini, Giannotti—unanimous concerning the general aims that the mixed government of a "well-
ordered republic" was meant to fulfill—held differing opinions
on the powers to be accorded to the various institutions. In
Guicciardini's view, the model Machiavelli proposed in his
Discourses, endowing the Extended Council with not only the
power to approve or reject laws but also the ability to propose
laws in free debate, was a source of "novelty and disturbance."
To ward off difficulties, he suggested that "nothing important
be left up to the people, save for those matters which, if left in
the hands of others, might endanger liberty itself, such as the
election of magistrates, while the creation of laws should not
be presented to the people, save after being considered and
approved by the supreme magistrates and by the senate; but
those laws that they develop should not take effect unless they
have been confirmed by the people."[13]

Giannotti, on the other hand, believed it was best for a
mixed republic to have a prevalence of the popular element. If
all the republic's components have the same weight, he
observed, each of them will try to prevail over the others,
engendering a state of permanent social and political instability. To keep this from happening, he suggested making one
component of the republic dominant over the others, on condition that it offer assurances not to use its power to impose a
partisan interest over the others and thus destroy liberty. The
only social component that could take on a dominant role in a
republic—in Giannotti's view, similar to Machiavelli's—was
the people.[14]

Despite their disagreements about the best way of ordering
a mixed government, republican theorists agreed that a good

government is one that prevents, through the separation of powers, the formation of arbitrary powers, whether of one alone, or a few, or many, that elude the rule of law. The unlimited power of the people is just as harmful as tyranny; the latter, wrote Machiavelli in his *Florentine Histories*, "displeases good men, the former displeases wise men; the latter can easily do harm, while the former can only do good with difficulty; in the latter, too much authority is given to insolent men, in the former too much authority is given to foolish men."[15] Machiavelli once again praised the political institutions of Lucca because the elders there, the Anziani, did *not* have "authority over the citizens." The reputation they enjoy as the highest executive power in the republic is already so great, wrote Machiavelli, "that if to that you add genuine authority, you will find that in short order ill effects will ensue."[16] Perhaps the republics of Italy were not able to achieve the separation of powers as well as eighteenth-century England did, but their republican theorists knew well, even without reading Montesquieu's *The Spirit of Laws*, that political liberty exists only where power is limited, by law and by other powers.

The Italian republics gave way to an era of principalities and foreign domination. After the fall of the last Florentine Republic in 1530, republicanism went through a complex process of transformation and adaptation to the political and intellectual context of the age of monarchies and principalities, a phase that has thus far received only scant attention from scholars.[17] Historical judgments on the transition from republics to monarchies vary according to whether the criterion of evaluation is the nation-state or self-government. Thinkers who saw the centralized monarchic state as an oppressive power depriving Italy's cities of autonomy and of the right to dispense as they wished the riches they had accumulated and saved considered the end of the republics as tantamount to the end of liberty. Those, like Antonio Gramsci, who saw the political problem of the modern era as being the formation of the modern territorial state hailed the decline of the republics as a step forward, agreeing on this point with those who, like Montesquieu, considered England's constitutional monarchy the form of government best suited to protect and nurture a modern commercial society.[18]

However, as Franco Venturi has demonstrated in his beautiful little book *Utopia and Reform in the Enlightenment*, it is a questionable historical judgment to assign to monarchies the role of being creator of the modern world and to consider republics as little more than museum relics, and republicanism itself on the order of an archaic critique of modernity. The seventeenth-century republics, notably the United Provinces of the Netherlands, could rightly boast of their entirely modern determination to establish peace, well-being, liberty, and tolerance in the face of the absolute monarchies' expansionism, power-mongering, and *raisons d'état*. Moreover, the republican tradition was one of the most important sources of the Enlightenment, the school of thought that more than any other contributed to the creation of the modern world. About mid-eighteenth-century France, Venturi wrote:

> Certainly a republican morale existed when the forms of state organization which had embodied it seemed antique and decaying ruins. There survived a republican friendship, a republican sense of duty, a republican pride, even though the world had changed. These may

even have existed in the very heart of a monarchical state, in the innermost self of those who seemed fully integrated in the world of absolutism. It is this ethical aspect of the republican tradition which appealed to the writers of the Enlightenment, to Voltaire, Diderot, d'Alembert, and, of course, to Rousseau. It mingled with the new vision of life being formed in mid-century Paris among the creators of the *Encyclopédie* on a moral, not a political level.[19]

During the French Revolution, in the view of some scholars, the republican ethos degenerated into an ideology that was critical of commercial society, insistent on the primacy of political will and on the radical dichotomy between liberty and despotism, and prone to considering every situation as a moment of crisis in which the political body was in danger of dissolving.[20] If indeed the Jacobins' republicanism did have these features, it is certain that its transformation from classical republicanism was quite substantial. In no classical republican work can we find a criticism of commercial society; indeed, praise of commerce, trades, banks, and the entrepreneurial spirit abounds. As for the idea that republicanism "metastasized" into the "language of terror," a single passage from Machiavelli's *Discourses* is enough to clarify the difference between Jacobin republicanism and classical republicanism. Machiavelli, discussing the transition from tyranny to liberty, is particularly instructive:

There one sees how much it is harmful to a republic or to a prince to hold the spirits of subjects in suspense and fearful with continued penalties and offenses. Without doubt one could not hold to a more pernicious order, because men who begin to suspect they have to suffer evil secure themselves by every mode in their dangers and become more audacious and less hesitant to try new things. Thus it is necessary either not to offend anyone ever or to do the offenses at a stroke, and then to reassure men and give them cause to quiet and steady their spirits.[21]

A republicanism that celebrates the primacy of political will, social and political cohesion, and terror has strayed greatly from its classical roots.

In the political and intellectual history of the nineteenth century, republicanism in France and England proceeded side by side with liberalism for long stretches during the formation and consolidation of their modern constitutional regimes. In Italy, primarily thanks to Mazzini's advocacy, republicanism became an ideal of independence and of equal civic and political dignity. While the classical republicans had thought that only some inhabitants of a city should have full political rights, Mazzini wanted the republic to be the city of all, in which no one—whether she was poor or of color—would feel like a stranger in her own country. For Mazzini, a true republic could not exclude the poor or women or blacks, and it had to ensure not only political equality but also the right to education and work if citizens were to acquire that sense of their own dignity that is proper to a genuine civic life.[22]

With Carlo Cattaneo, who was fond of quoting the passage in which Machiavelli explained that "a people, in order to preserve its liberty, must keep it firmly in its hands," republicanism became a federalist theory of political liberty. Cattaneo believed, in fact, that a people could preserve its liberty only by means of self-government, and he identified a republic with liberty. "Liberty," he wrote, "is republic"—but he added, and it is an important addition, "Republic is plurality, which is to say, federation." He meant by this, as Norberto Bobbio observed, that "the unified state, by its very nature, cannot help being authoritarian and thus in the end imperious and despotic, because unity tends in and of itself to suffocate autonomy, free initiative, in a word, liberty; and it is only a plurality of political centers, or perhaps we should say, only a pluralistic, non-undifferentiated unity, a unity with variety as opposed to a unity without distinctions, that offers any real assurance of liberty; this is the only environment in which society can prosper and make civic progress."[23] Moreover, Cattaneo rightly believed that Italian history itself, in its most vital aspects, tended toward the federal republic: "But this is proper to our nation, that the republican soul is found in all orders . . . and indeed it seems that outside of this form of government our nation does not know how to achieve great things."[24]

The New Utopia
of Liberty

R EPUBLICANISM NOT ONLY IS a noble tradition of the past but also is meant as a new, or rediscovered, utopia of political liberty. Theorists of republicanism today claim that true political liberty consists not only of the absence of interference (in the actions that individuals wish to perform and are capable of performing) from other individuals or institutions, as liberals claim, but also of the absence of domination (or dependence), understood as the condition of the individual who does not have to depend on the arbitrary will of other individuals or institutions that might oppress him or her with impunity if they so desired.[1]

A few examples can help to clarify the difference between being subject to interference, or hindered, and being dependent, or subject to domination. Let us consider the following cases: citizens who can be oppressed by a tyrant or an oligarchy that has no fear of incurring legally prescribed sanctions; a wife who can be abused by her husband without being able to resist or to demand restitution; workers who can be subjected to minor or major abuses from their employer or supervisor; a retiree who must depend on the whim of a functionary to obtain the pension to which he has a legitimate right; an invalid who must depend on the goodwill of a physician in order to get well; young scholars who know that their careers depend not on the quality of their work but on the whims of a senior professor; a citizen who can be thrown into prison at the arbitrary word of a magistrate. In all these cases there is no *interference*: I spoke not of a tyrant or oligarchy that oppresses but of one that *can* oppress if it chooses; I said not that the husband abuses his wife but that he *can* abuse her without fear of sanction, and the same goes for the employer, the functionary, the physician, the professor, and the judge. None of them keeps others from pursuing the ends they wish to pursue; none of them interferes in the lives of others. The subjects—the wife, the workers, the retiree, the invalid, the young scholars—are thus perfectly free if by freedom we mean freedom from interference or freedom—and this amounts to the same thing—from hindrance or restriction. They are subject, however, to the arbitrary will of other individuals and therefore live in a condition of dependence, like the slaves of whom Plautus writes in his comedies, who are often perfectly free to do what they want, either because their master is far away or because he is kind or foolish, but who are also subject to his arbitrary will, since he can punish them harshly if he chooses.

While interference is an action or an obstacle to action, dependence is a conditioning of the will that has fear as its distinguishing feature. A fine description of dependence as a denial of liberty, and the fear it engenders, has been given by Francesco Mario Pagano:

> If the law supplies the means, either to a private citizen or to an entire class and branch of the state or to the magistrate himself, for oppressing others with the forces of public order, which are required to defend everyone equally, through an act not merely of omission but indeed of commission, civil liberty is suffocated. Not just the *deed* but the mere *ability* to do it, even if no violence is entailed, is an offense against liberty. Freedom is so very fragile that every shadow darkens it, the slightest breath fogs it over. The mere belief that one *might be oppressed with impunity* strips us of the free faculty to avail ourselves of our rights. Fear attacks liberty at its very source. It is a poison steeped in the spring whence flows the river—there, where external force hinders only the exercise of liberty.[2]

An equally clear description of political liberty as the absence of fear can be found in *The Spirit of Laws*: "The political liberty of the subject is a tranquility of mind, arising from the opinion each person has of his safety. In order to have this liberty, it is requisite the government be so constituted as one man need not be afraid of another."[3]

Having clarified the difference between interference and dependence, or domination, we need add that there is interference without domination when we are subjected to the restraints and restrictions of law. A law that requires that I and all other citizens pay taxes in proportion to our income, or a law that condemns me and anyone else to a life sentence if we commit murder, to name two obvious examples, certainly constitutes a restraint, restriction, or interference, but it does not make me in any way dependent on the arbitrary will of other people, because these are restrictions given not to me in particular but to one and all and they do not express the will of one or more persons imposing their personal interest. As Rousseau put it, "One is always free when one is subject to the laws, but not when one must obey another man; because in the latter case I must obey the will of another."[4]

Does this interpretation of political liberty as the absence of dependence, which neo-republican theorists propose, introduce a significant new feature into our political language? Two canonical texts of the liberal doctrine of political liberty—Benjamin Constant's "Discourse on the Liberty of the Ancients Compared with That of the Moderns" and Isaiah Berlin's "Two Concepts of Liberty"—do not mention the idea of liberty as the absence of personal dependence. Constant distinguishes between liberty in antiquity—which consisted "in exercising collectively but directly many functions of the entire sovereignty, deliberating on war and peace in the public square, concluding treaties of alliance with foreigners, voting on laws, handing down judgments, managing magistrates, having them appear before the entire populace, placing them under accusation, condemning them, or absolving them"—and liberty in modernity, which consists of

> the right to be subjected only to the laws, and to be
> neither arrested, detained, put to death or maltreated

in any way by the arbitrary will of one or more individuals. It is the right of everyone to express their opinion, choose a profession and practise it, to dispose of property, and even to abuse it; to come and go without permission, and without having to account for their motives or undertakings. It is everyone's right to associate with other individuals, either to discuss their interests, or to profess the religion which they and their associates prefer, or even simply to occupy their days or hours in a way which is most compatible with their inclinations or whims. Finally it is everyone's right to exercise some influence on the administration of the government, either by electing all or particular officials, or through representations, petitions, demands to which the authorities are more or less compelled to pay heed.

Berlin takes Constant's idea and makes a distinction between negative and positive liberty. The first, he writes, can be described thus:

I am normally said to be free to the degree to which no man or body of men interferes with my activity. Political liberty in this sense is simply the area within which a man can act unobstructed by others . . . Freedom in this sense is not, at any rate logically, connected with democracy or self-government. Self-government may, on the whole, provide a better guarantee of the preservation of civil liberties than other regimes, and has been defended as such by libertarians. But there is no necessary connection between individual liberty and democratic rule.

Positive liberty is different:

> The "positive" sense of the word "liberty" derives from the wish on the part of the individual to be his own master. I wish my life and decisions to depend on myself, not on external forces of whatever kind. I wish to be the instrument of my own, not of other men's, acts of will. I wish to be a subject, not an object; to be moved by reasons, by conscious purposes, which are my own, not by causes which affect me, as it were, from outside.[5]

As legitimate as this wish may be, claims Berlin, the positive conception of liberty has historically been viewed as the affirmation of a true, or superior, or autonomous "ego" that should be allowed to triumph over all, even if through coercion. For this reason, liberals have thought of the positive idea of liberty as a mask concealing tyranny.

It is easy to see that the republican conception of liberty is neither the negative nor the positive liberty described by Berlin and Constant. Republican liberty differs from its liberal counterpart in that it identifies the absence of liberty not merely in interference (being obstructed by others, as Berlin puts it) but in the *constant possibility* of interference due to the presence of arbitrary powers. No republican political writer would call liberty a "liberty" enjoyed by subjects of a "liberal" despot, as Berlin does, since the despot could, at any time and at his own discretion, keep them from doing what they want to do and might otherwise oppress them. They are subject to no interference, but they are in a condition of dependence: a liberal can describe it as a condition of liberty, but a republican cannot. Nor can a republican identify liberty as the affirmation of a certain type of life or self; to speak of liberty it is sufficient for there to be an absence of domination, whatever the way of life the person chooses and whatever self she wishes to affirm.

Both Constant and Berlin identify modern, or negative, liberty as the fundamental or more genuine form of liberty, even if they admit that liberty understood as active participation in public life can have positive effects on the defense of modern liberty. Neither—and this is the point I wish to emphasize—treats an absence of personal dependence as important to political liberty. It is not necessary here to ask why Constant and Berlin overlooked a conception of political liberty that stretches back over centuries and that has been analyzed and debated in many fundamental texts. But their silence on this point is surprising: if they chose not to discuss the republican idea of liberty because they considered it irrelevant or identical to negative or positive liberty, they might have said so; if they overlooked it out of ignorance, it is further confirmation that those who reason about political theory with inadequate historical knowledge rarely develop theories of great importance.

The republican conception of liberty differs from the democratic idea that liberty consists of the "power to establish norms for oneself and to obey no other norms than those given to oneself." This is liberty in the sense of autonomy. Democratic liberty, as Bobbio puts it, is opposed to *constraint*. A person who is free in the democratic sense of the word is therefore a person who has free *will*: the "nonconformist who thinks for himself, who waits for approval from no one, who withstands pressure, flattery, and illusory career goals," who, in other words, has a free will in the sense that he enjoys self-determination.

The democratic conception of liberty also differs from the liberal conception, in which, as Bobbio explains, "one speaks of liberty as something in contrast to the law, to all forms of law, so that all laws (both prohibitive and imperative) restrict liberty." In the democratic conception, "one speaks of liberty as a field of action in compliance with the law, and one distinguishes not between an unregulated action and an action regulated by the law, but rather between an action regulated by an autonomous law (one accepted voluntarily) and an action regulated by a heteronomous law (one accepted under duress)."[6]

The republican conception of political liberty approaches the democratic idea of liberty as autonomy of the will in that it, too, sees constraint as a violation of liberty; yet it is not identical, because it holds that the will is autonomous not when the laws or regulations that govern my actions correspond to my will, but when I am protected from the *constant danger* of being subjected to constraint. Republican political writers have never claimed that liberty consists of actions regulated by law (that is, accepted voluntarily) or of the power to bestow rules or to follow only the rules we give ourselves; instead, they have claimed that the power to make laws for ourselves—directly or through representatives—is the efficacious means (along with others) for living free, in the sense of not being subject to the arbitrary will of one or a few or many individuals.

Action regulated by law is free, in other words, not when the law is accepted voluntarily, or when it corresponds to the desires of the citizens, but when the law is not arbitrary, that is, when it respects universal norms (when it applies to all individuals or to all members of the group in question), aspires to the public good, and for this reason protects the will of the citizens from the constant danger of constraint imposed by individuals and therefore renders the will fully autonomous. A law accepted voluntarily by members of the most democratic assembly on earth may very well be an arbitrary law that permits some part of the society to constrain the will of other parts, thus depriving them of their autonomy.

The republican conception of liberty, then, is more exacting than either the liberal or the democratic conception: it accepts the idea of liberty as an absence of impediment, but it adds the requirement that liberty be an absence of domination (of the constant possibility of interference); it accepts the democratic requirement of self-determination as a means to obtaining liberty, but it does not identify self-government with the political liberty consistent with a republic. Republicanism sustains a complex theory of political liberty that incorporates both the liberal and the democratic requirement; conversely, we can say that liberalism and democracy are impoverished versions of republicanism. On this last point, given its theoretical and political importance, it would be worthwhile to spend a little more time.

THREE

The Value of
Republican Liberty

NEO-REPUBLICAN THEORISTS DISAGREE over the
meaning of republican liberty. In his first essays on
the subject, Quentin Skinner said that republican
political writers and liberal theorists agree on the meaning of
political liberty, which both identify as the absence of coercion
or interference, but differ on the political conditions that make
liberty secure. In a later essay on the subject, *Liberty before
Liberalism*, he maintains instead that the difference between
liberal and republican theorists (or between liberal theorists
and the neo-Roman political writers of the seventeenth and
eighteenth centuries, as he calls them, because they were not
all advocates of republican government) is to be found not in
their views of what secures political liberty but in their differing interpretations of what constitutes a restraint or constraint.
Neo-Roman political authors, he thinks, accept unreservedly
the idea that the citizens' degree of liberty depends on the

measure to which they are restrained in the actions they wish to take in pursuing their aims. They repudiate, in other words, "the key assumption of classical liberalism to the effect that force or the coercive threat of it constitute the only forms of constraint that interfere with individual liberty." They emphasize, rather, that "to live in a condition of dependence is in itself a source and a form of constraint." An individual who lives in a condition of dependence is subject to a constraint that prevents him from exercising his civil rights. The absence of liberty can be caused, then, he concludes, "by interference or by dependence."[1]

According to Philip Pettit, the absence of liberty is, rather, the consequence of dependence (or domination). Interference and constraints, including those imposed by nonarbitrary laws, should be considered only a "secondary offense against freedom." In other words, while Skinner believes that republican liberty includes the absence both of domination and of interference, Pettit agrees but adds that the absence of interference is the less relevant violation. He emphasizes that it is difficult to find in republican political writers a significant critique of the limitation on freedom of choice that the rule of law imposes on individuals. They accept the restrictions on freedom of choice and emphasize the difference between the conditions of those living under the rule of law and those living or wanting to live in a condition of limitless license. Republican political writers have always shown complete scorn for license and have always emphasized that license and civil liberty are two quite different matters. They never considered that restrictions on freedom of choice imposed by the rule of law might be construed as "a serious infringement on liberty."[2]

Both Skinner and Pettit reject the idea that being free means obeying laws that we ourselves have approved, and they both emphasize that the republican or neo-Roman conception of political freedom is not a positive conception of liberty consisting in the direct exercise of political rights. But while Skinner believes that the absence of liberty "can be produced either by interference or by dependence,"[3] Pettit believes that it consists solely of dependence.

I think it is important to emphasize in this debate that classical republican writers have never claimed that true political liberty consists of the absence of interference, since they believed that restraint or interference which the law imposes on individual choice was not a restraint on liberty but a brake, an essential limitation intrinsic to republican liberty. (In contrast, Isaiah Berlin noted that "Bentham, almost alone, doggedly went on repeating that the business of laws was not to liberate but to restrain: 'Every law is an infraction of liberty'—even if such 'infraction' leads to an increase to the sum of liberty."[4]) They considered the law a public and universal commandment that applied equally to all citizens or to all members of the group in question. This meant that if the rule of law was scrupulously respected, no individual could impose his arbitrary will on other individuals by performing with impunity actions forbidden to others under pain of sanction. If men govern instead of laws, some individuals can impose their wills on others, oppressing them or keeping them from pursuing the ends they wish to pursue, and thus depriving them of liberty. (This can also be true in a case where the majority rules, that is, in a democracy.)

This interpretation of political liberty is eloquently described in three classical texts that are the core of modern republicanism. The first is Livy's statement that the liberty the Romans regained after the expulsion of the kings consisted, first and foremost, in having the laws be more powerful than men. The second is the speech, reported by Sallust, in which Aemilius Lepidus proclaimed that the Roman people were free because they obeyed no one but their own laws. The third is the passage from Cicero's *Pro Cluentio*, quoted countless times by political writers in the Renaissance and later: "All of us obey the law to the end that we may be free."[5]

A second aspect of the republican conception of political liberty is the conviction that liberty entails restraints or brakes (*frenum*) on individual actions. These two aspects of Roman political wisdom were adopted and reformulated by Florentine civic humanists. Liberty, wrote Coluccio Salutati, is a "gentle brake" ("*dulce libertatis frenum*") that the law imposes on all citizens. Leonardo Bruni reiterated the same principle: true liberty ("*mera ac vera Libertas*") consists of the equality guaranteed by the laws. And he attributes to Giano della Bella the idea that liberty is preserved ("*Libertas servatur*") so long as the laws are more powerful than the citizens. In the late fifteenth century, it was primarily opponents of the Medici who emphasized that the foundation of civil liberty was the rule of law: a republic that wishes to "live in liberty," wrote Alamanno Rinuccini, must not allow a citizen "to be more powerful than the laws."[6]

Machiavelli, too, identified the liberty of citizens with the restrictions the law imposes equally on them all. If in a city there is one citizen whom the magistrates fear, who can therefore break the bonds of the laws, then that city is not free, he wrote in the *Discourses*. In the *Florentine Histories* he wrote that a city "can be called free" only if its laws and constitutional provisions efficaciously restrain the bad impulses of the nobility and the populace. And by civil liberty he meant the absence of domination or dependence: "Without doubt, if one considers the ends of the nobles and of the ignobles, one will see great desire to dominate in the former, and in the latter only desire not to be dominated; and, in consequence, a greater will to live free."[7]

In contrast, all the instances of violation of liberty that the classical republicans offer are violations of the rule of law: a tyrant who sets himself above civil and constitutional laws and therefore rules by whim; a powerful citizen who has obtained for himself a privilege denied to other citizens and who can therefore do things that others cannot (such as use public resources for private gain or obtain public offices in violation of normal procedures); a ruler who has discretionary powers. The restrictions that law imposes on the actions of rulers and ordinary citizens are considered the only valid defense against coercion by individuals. To be free means living under equitable laws.

As for the relationship between liberty and self-government, the classical republicans considered the latter a condition of the former. For Roman political writers, a people who receives its laws from a king is enslaved, not free; it lives in a state not of liberty but of servitude, similar to that of a slave with respect to his master.[8] Absolute monarchy is therefore similar to domination, while the republic is the form of government and way of life of a free people.

Republican government, as Machiavelli explained in a passage of enlightening lucidity, is best suited to the defense of liberty because it has the power to prevent private interests from dominating the city and rendering some, or many, citizens unfree: "And without doubt this common good is not observed if not in republics, since all that is for that purpose is executed, and although it may turn out to harm this or that private individual, those for whom the aforesaid does good are so many that they can go ahead with it against the disposition of the few who are crushed by it."[9] But Machiavelli also explains that there can be laws that comply with the citizens' will and desires but that impose a private interest and therefore destroy political liberty. As an example, he mentions the agrarian law that the Roman plebeians, "through ambition," called for, which "was the cause of the destruction of the republic" and "altogether ruined Roman freedom."[10]

The republican argument that the rule of law is a necessary condition for citizens to live free and to prevent them from being subject to the arbitrary will of a few individuals (or a single individual) is at the heart of James Harrington's reply to Hobbes's claim in *Leviathan* that the citizens of a republic such as Lucca had no more freedom than the subjects of an absolute sovereign such as the sultan of Constantinople, because both were subject to laws. What makes the citizens of Lucca freer than the subjects of Constantinople, Harrington argues, is that in Lucca both rulers and citizens are subject to civil and constitutional laws, whereas in Constantinople the sultan is above the law and may arbitrarily dispose of the property and lives of his subjects, obliging them to live in a condition of complete dependence and therefore without liberty. The citizens of Lucca, Harrington explains, are free "by the laws of Lucca," because they are controlled only by the law and because the laws are "framed by every private man unto no other end . . . than to protect the liberty of every private man, which by that means comes to be the liberty of the commonwealth."[11]

The idea that the rule of law protects a citizen from the arbitrary will of others because it binds everyone in the same way passed from the books of republican theorists to those written by the founders of liberalism. The most significant example is that of John Locke:

> *The end of Law* is not to abolish or restrain, but *to preserve and enlarge Freedom*: For in all the states of created beings capable of Laws, *where there is no Law, there is no Freedom*. For *Liberty* is to be free from restraint and violence from others which cannot be, where there is no Law: But Freedom is not, as we are told, *A Liberty for every Man to do what he lists*: (For who could be free, when every other Man's Humour might domineer over him?) But a *Liberty* to dispose, and order, as he lists, his Person, Actions, Possessions, and his whole Property, within the Allowance of those Laws under which he is; and therein not to be subject to the arbitrary Will of another, but freely follow his own.[12]

The limitation that law imposes on the decisions of individuals differs from the limitation that an individual might arbitrarily impose on others: in the first case, we have obedience, in the second case, servitude.

The passages quoted here make it clear that republican political writers never identified as limitations on liberty the restraints imposed by nonarbitrary laws, but they have always defined as such any dependence on the arbitrary will of other individuals. They believed that the rule of law makes individuals free, not because it expresses their own will—not, that is, because they have given their assent to it—but because the law is a universal and abstract command and as such protects individuals from the arbitrary will of others. For them, the validity of various institutional systems is measured by their efficacy in preventing the arbitrary use of power. When Machiavelli defended the virtues of republican government, he always referred to that government in which the functions of power were distributed according to the model of mixed government, where the people exercised sovereign power within the limits defined by constitutional law.

While it is certainly legitimate to consider dependence on the arbitrary will of an individual "a source and a form of constraint,"[13] as Skinner does, I believe that making a distinction between dependence on arbitrary will and subjection to restraint offers the best insight into classical republicanism's conception of political liberty. If it is to have any significance in contemporary discussions, neo-republicanism must show that it is critical of dependence and domination, and it must sharply differentiate itself from both laissez-faire intolerance of restraints and authoritarian insensitivity toward domination.

Classical republicanism has always opposed dependence because it believes that this encourages servility on the one hand and arrogance on the other, two mentalities that are equally repugnant to the ideal of civil life. This is particularly important because the persistence of arbitrary powers and of practices of domination, as well as license and the absence of moral and social responsibility, suffocates civil culture. Democratic societies need a political and moral language that can illustrate persuasively the significance and value of a dignified civil life. In this regard, republicanism has authoritative credentials, provided it remains faithful to the aversion its masters felt for both tyranny and license.

A further reason for distinguishing between being subject to restraints and being dependent is that legislative measures that free some citizens from dependence restrict others in their freedom to act. Consider some of the examples cited at the beginning of Chapter 2: a wife who cannot offer resistance to or demand restitution for abuse by her husband; workers who may be subjected to abuse from their employer or supervisor; the elderly, the sick, and those living alone who depend on charity. To free women from dependence, one must have laws that ensure equality within the family, limiting the arbitrary power of men; to protect dependent workers, one must have laws that safeguard their physical and moral dignity and limit their employer's arbitrary power; to emancipate the needy from charity, one must impose taxes that provide adequate public assistance. In these cases, reducing the domination from which some citizens suffer entails increasing the restriction of others' (negative) liberty; or, rather, it requires imposing restraints on individuals who once could act of their own free will. It is not possible to reduce dependence without imposing legal restraints. We must choose between domination (and dependence) and the restraint of the law. Those who hark back to republican tradition must choose policies that attenuate domination rather than those that try to attenuate civic obligation in the guise of being free from impediments.

This does not mean that republicans should not appreciate liberty as the absence of interference or of constraints. Nor does it mean that they should consider it a liberty of lesser value or dignity than liberty as the absence of dependence.[14] It means only that if liberty as the absence of domination for some conflicts with liberty as the absence of restraint or interference for others, then we must place the former above the latter, since that is more in keeping with the ideal of the *res publica*, a community of individuals in which no one is forced to serve and no one is allowed to dominate, an ideal that has been and remains the core of the republican utopia.

The most perceptive republican theorists point out that questions of liberty are controversial ones that can be answered only in ways that some will hail and others condemn. They understand that the common good is neither the good (or interest) of everyone nor a good (or interest) that transcends private interests; rather, it is the good of citizens who wish to live free and independent and as such is opposed to the good of those who wish to dominate. This interpretation should answer some of the concerns raised by feminist scholars. "When republicanism gets associated with ideals of transcendence," wrote Ann Phillips, for example, "with the notion that citizens must set aside their partial, parochial, one-sided preoccupations to address issues of a general nature, many will ask what guarantee there is that women's interests and preoccupations will be incorporated into the general good."[15]

Precisely because republican theorists do not believe that the common good is the good of each and all, they do not fear social and political conflicts, as long as those conflicts remain within the boundaries of civil life, and they appreciate the value of the clashes of rhetoric that occur in public councils. They do not foster the notion of an organic community where individuals work toward a common good, nor do they waste time fantasizing about republics where laws aspiring to the common good are approved unanimously by virtuous citizens.

Contemporary republican theorists should learn from the wisdom of their classical forerunners and think of disputes over political liberty as conflicts between partisan interests and conceptions, not as philosophical debates whose goal it is to ascertain or demonstrate the truth. Determining what constitutes an arbitrary action or what it means to be subjected to the arbitrary will of an individual—two determinations that are essential to any identification of domination—cannot help being partisan and questionable.

Evaluations of all political actions tend to be partisan, subjective, driven by passions; disputes in the real world are neither scientific nor philosophical but, rather, rhetorical in the classical sense of the term. That the state should impose taxes proportional to income in order to ensure decent health care and good schools for needy citizens, for example, will be viewed by some citizens as an entirely arbitrary interference, indeed even a full-fledged act of tyranny; to others it will constitute a legitimate instance of interference. No facts can be cited to settle the debate definitively and objectively, nor will it ever be possible to establish procedures that enable us to resolve the debate in such a way that all contending parties are satisfied.

FOUR

Republicanism, Liberalism, and Communitarianism

To LIVE UP TO ITS AMBITION to be a major intellectual and political framework for constitutional democracies, modern republicanism must clearly state its
own position with respect to other schools of contemporary
political thought, especially liberalism. The intellectual challenge it poses for liberalism is relatively new. Throughout its
long history, liberalism has been criticized in the name of justice, in the name of social hierarchy and tradition, in the name
of ideals of moral renewal and perfection, in the name of communitarian ideals, or in the name of a more broadly based participation in sovereign power—but almost never in the name
of liberty, its fundamental principle (except when it has been
challenged in the name of "true" or "substantial" liberty as distinct from formal liberty).[1] Liberalism has been formidably
successful in defending individuals against the interference of
the state or other individuals, but less so in accommodating

the demands for liberty voiced by men and women who must keep their eyes cast down—or wide open to ascertain the moods of the powerful people who with impunity may at any time force them to obey, even to serve them. When liberals have wanted to struggle against this kind of domination, they have been unable to deploy a concept of liberty as an absence of interference, clearly unsuited to the purpose, and have had to allude to other ideals, such as justice or equality (hence the various hybrid terms, perfectly nice in their way: "justice and liberty," "liberal socialism," "social liberalism").

From a historical point of view, the relationship of liberalism to republicanism is one of derivation and innovation. Liberalism is a doctrine derived from republicanism in the sense that it has taken several of its fundamental principles from republicanism, notably that of the defense of the limited state against the absolute state. It is true, as the liberal Norberto Bobbio writes, that all the theorists to whom the liberal conception of the state is attributed insist on the necessity of limiting the supreme power, but it is equally true that republican political theorists affirm the same requirement with equal energy both for republics and for monarchical governments. Machiavelli, for one, calls absolute power "tyranny" and explains elsewhere that "a prince who can do what he wishes is crazy; a people that can do what it wishes is not wise."[2]

Liberalism is an individualistic political theory which states that the chief objective of a political community is to protect the life, liberty, and property of its individual members. Liberals rightly boast of the excellence of this principle when debating with communitarians, who set the objective as the affirmation of some concept of moral good; or with theocrats, who believe the goal is the pursuit of salvation; or with organicists, who see it as the good of society at large, or the group, or the nation. But this central liberal tenet was earlier set forth by republican theorists. Cicero, in *De officiis* (II.21.73), claims that the security of property was the first reason men abandoned the condition of natural liberty and established political communities.[3] When Machiavelli explains what constitutes the "common utility that comes from a free way of life," he mentions no collective goal and emphasizes that it consists in "being able to enjoy one's things freely and without any worries, not fearing for the honor of wives and children, not fearing for oneself."[4]

Liberals are especially right to claim—against conservative doctrines of social harmony or the Marxist utopia of a pacific and pacified society—that social conflict is both inevitable and indeed beneficial. But credit for this pearl of political wisdom goes to Machiavelli; it appears with all the power of innovation in his *Discourses*, where he explains that social conflicts in Republican Rome between plebeians and the Senate "were the first cause of keeping Rome free."[5] Those who rightly admire John Stuart Mill for his criticism of conformity and praise of diversity should admire all the more the pages in which Machiavelli praises the variety of the world and underscores that everyone should live in his or her own way and not in the manner of others. Some republicans have thought of the republic as a New Jerusalem in which morality and virtue reign, and others have supported the necessity of censorship and civil religion, but classical republicanism wasted no time or energy on such fantasies of moral and spiritual improvement.

Things are different where the principle of the division or separation of powers is concerned. Even though liberal theorists have gone much further with this theme than have the masters of classical republicanism, it is all the same true, as I have already suggested, that the republican writers made a clear distinction among the various functions of sovereignty (legislative, executive, and judicial powers).

The doctrine of natural (or innate, or inalienable) rights proper to classical liberalism may have played a fundamental part in the defense of individual liberty and in the emancipation of peoples and groups, but it suffers from a theoretical weakness which liberal theorists themselves have pointed out. Rights are in fact only rights if custom or law recognizes them as such and are therefore always historical, not natural; and if they are not historical and not recognized by law, then they are only moral aspirations, unquestionably very important, but nothing more than moral aspirations.

Similarly, the various theories about the social contract—which see the fundamental norms that regulate political institutions as being the product of a consensus that individuals achieve in certain (ideal) conditions of choice—do not claim to have explicative value, to explain how states are formed, but only normative value, that is, showing why it is better to live in a state than not and why one type of state is better than another. Though there have been republican political theorists of the social contract (Rousseau, to name one), the doctrine is ill suited, in my view, to republicanism. I believe it is wiser to elaborate normative arguments on the value of political constitutions by using history to compare past with present or the institutions of one country with those of another. This avoids the awkwardness of having to shift from an ideal model to the political and social reality we are trying to understand, and it allows us to endow our reasoning with the persuasive force of

examples and narration. Republican political language originated and developed primarily in the councils of free republics, where after debate sovereign decisions were made; it is a
language of rhetoric rather than of philosophy; it seeks not
truth but the common good; it requires not abstract foundations but wisdom.

We can at least posit that from a historical point of view
liberalism owes to classical republicanism its most valid doc-
trinal principles, while those principles it owes to itself have
withstood the test of time less well. And it has only itself, or
some of its masters, to blame for its forgetting the republican
conception of political liberty and thus having weakened, as I
have said, its capacity to accommodate the demands of liberty
as the absence of dependence, which are central to the ideal of
civil liberty.

From a theoretical point of view, liberalism can be considered an impoverished or incoherent republicanism, but not an
alternative to republicanism. If, as Quentin Skinner argues,
republicans, unlike liberals, insist that "to live in a condition of
dependence is in and of itself a cause and a form of constraint," then republicanism is a liberal theory that is more radical and consistent than classical liberalism. While liberals
believe that "force or the coercive threat of it constitute the
only form of constraint that interferes with individual liberty"
(emphasis mine), republicans want to reduce as much as possible the constraint that weighs on individuals and for this reason also are willing to struggle against the forms of constraint
that derive from dependence.

If we accept Pettit's thesis that republicanism considers
domination, not constraint, the principal enemy of liberty,
then we can assert that a liberal considers that all laws (even

nonarbitrary ones that aim to reduce the dependence of certain citizens on the arbitrary will of others) restrict liberty,
while a republican considers the same laws the most secure
bulwark protecting liberty and is therefore willing to accept
even severe interference if that reduces the weight of arbitrary
power and domination over himself and others. This interpretation makes republicanism incompatible with libertarian
ideologies, though not with liberalism. Many liberals agree
with the republican objective of expanding liberty beyond its
present boundaries. Republicans would like more women and
men to share the culture of citizenship; consider democratic
equality a fine and worthy thing; refuse to be anyone's servant
but treat everyone with respect; stand ready to fulfill their civic
duties and practice solidarity. Expanding the boundaries of liberty means seeing to it that fewer men and women must
depend on the arbitrary judgment of others in order to have
careers, whether in the public or private sector; that fewer and
fewer citizens feel defenseless in the face of public authority
and bureaucracy; that fewer and fewer citizens are forced into
silence or passivity because their social or cultural or ethnic
group is considered inferior, their history without value; that
fewer and fewer citizens are discriminated against or treated
arrogantly or condescendingly in the workplace, or confined—
even self-confined—to the inner spaces of domestic life. Why
should liberals oppose these aspirations to greater liberty? If
liberals incorporated the ideal of liberty as absence of domination into their language and politics, they would instill new
vigor into their political message for the new century.[6]

Skinner has noted the important theoretical difference
between classical republicanism and liberalism in the lan-

guage of rights. Classical republicans, Machiavelli first among them, fail to speak of rights, much less of innate or natural rights. (Of course, there are authoritative liberal theorists who also do not presume the idea of innate or natural rights.[7]) Still, it is important to point out that the modern idea of rights is perfectly consistent with republican ideals of political liberty and civil life. The idea and, especially, the practice of rights teach citizens a way of life that rejects both servility and arrogance, as Tocqueville explained in a passage rich in classical republican echoes:

> Next to virtue as a general idea, nothing, I think, is so beautiful as that of rights, and indeed the two ideas are mingled. The idea of rights is nothing but the conception of virtue applied to the world of politics.
>
> By means of the idea of rights men have defined the nature of license and of tyranny. Guided by its light, we can each of us be independent without arrogance and obedient without servility. When a man submits to force, that surrender debases him; but when he accepts the recognized right of a fellow mortal to give him orders, there is a sense in which he rises above the giver of the commands. No man can be great without virtue, nor any nation great without respect for rights; one might almost say that without it there can be no society, for what is a combination of rational and intelligent beings held together by force alone?[8]

The major convergences between liberalism and republicanism notwithstanding, the republican ideal of liberty is, I believe, more useful to contemporary democracies than the liberal one. It enables us to identify dependence on the arbitrary will of one or more individuals as a loss of liberty and above all to show clearly and more persuasively the link between liberty and civic virtue. A person who subscribes to the ideal of liberty as the mere absence of interference can agree to perform certain civic duties—giving money to charitable institutions, supporting programs of social solidarity, participating in groups that are characteristic of civil society— either because she believes these actions have a moral value, or that they help to keep the community decent and tranquil, or that a commitment to the public good (patriotism, to use Benjamin Constant's term) helps to protect individual liberty from the abuses of arrogant rulers and citizens. Still, it would be very difficult to persuade such a person to agree to be required by law to give money or time to works in the common interest, since she would see that as a limitation of liberty. Liberal liberty is not merely the absence of interference but also "immunity from service," as Hobbes writes in *Leviathan*. But citizens who accept the republican ideal of liberty do not agree, because they identify a lack of liberty differently. Unlike liberals, who consider public service a restriction on liberty, they consider it a natural companion to liberty. To hark back to Hobbes once again, they know that the citizens of Lucca are required to serve the public good to a much greater extent than are the subjects of the sultan in Constantinople, but they know they would feel freer in Lucca.

However important the differences between republicanism and liberalism, those separating republicanism from the various communitarian philosophies are even more marked, proposing as they do to reinforce the moral and cultural unity of our democratic societies as a means of reviving civic virtue. Yet the belief that republicanism is a form of communitarianism is widespread in international political theory. Jürgen Habermas, for example, has written that republicanism is an intellectual tradition derived from Aristotle based on the principle of citizenship as membership in an ethnic and cultural community that enjoys self-government. In his view, republicanism considers citizens parts of the community who can develop and express their own identity and moral excellence only within a shared tradition and culture that include a conception of moral goodness.[9]

This interpretation of republicanism as a form of political Aristotelianism is a historiographical error. Republican theorists believed that being a citizen meant not so much belonging to a self-governing ethno-cultural community as exercising the civil and political rights that derived from belonging to a *res publica*, or *civitas*, that is, a *political* community, whose goal was to allow individuals to live together in justice and liberty under the rule of law. For republicans, the most important common good was justice, because it is only in a just republic that individuals do not have to serve the will of others and can live freely. The basis of the republic is therefore the very idea of equal rights or justice that communitarian philosophers try to enrich with a shared conception of moral good.

For republican political writers, the republic is not an abstract political reality but a good that our forefathers helped to build and that it is our task to preserve if we want those who come after us to live in freedom. Every national community is special, and it has *its own* history and *its own* character which make it different from others, but in order to be a true republic, it must be based on justice. A republic founded on justice and the rule of law can supply the friendship, solidarity, and belonging that communitarians speak about. But a republic built on a particular conception of goodness, on a particular culture, will not be a republic for everyone, and it will therefore not be just.

Another contemporary error is the idea that republicanism considers participation in self-government the highest value.[10] As I have already observed, classical republican theorists believed that participation in the life of the republic was important both to preserve liberty and to give civic education to its citizens, and therefore that it should be encouraged in all reasonable ways. But it was not the main value or objective of the republic; it was a means to protect liberty and to select the best citizens for positions of responsibility. It is often more important to have good rulers than to have citizens participate in every decision. What counts is that those who govern and decide wish to serve the common good.

Republican equality does not consist solely of equality of civil and political rights; it also affirms the need to ensure all citizens the social, economic, and cultural conditions to allow them to live with dignity and self-respect. The masters of modern republicanism left us two particularly valuable considerations on this theme of social equality. The first, formulated by Machiavelli, is that poverty should not translate into either exclusion from public honors or a loss of repute. The second, which we owe to Rousseau, is that in a republic worthy of the name no one should be so poor as to be forced to sell himself (or to sell his loyalty and obedience to powerful and wealthy citizens, becoming a servant or a client) or so rich as to be able to purchase, with favors, the obedience of other citizens.

These two principles form the fundamental underpinnings of republican equality in our times. The first requires that our government not allow poverty to close the doors to public and private careers or to education. It must do this for reasons of justice, because the republic cannot tolerate a situation in which citizens have to undergo the humiliating experience of exclusion and because the republic must want the best people, not the richest or the most privileged ones, to win out in competition for honors and distinction; indeed, precisely because it needs the best to win out, it must require that the competition be fair.

The second principle, that of Rousseau, requires that the republic ensure that everyone has the right to work and the social rights that will keep him or her from hitting bottom when misfortune strikes. These social rights should not, however, be confused with the welfare-state approach, which risks creating lifelong clients of the state, sanctions certain privileges, and fails to encourage individuals to help themselves. Nor should they be confused with public (or, worse, private) charity, which offers aid as an act of goodwill. Public (and private) charity, however praiseworthy, is incompatible with civil life because it offends the dignity of those who receive it. To be sick or old is no crime. A republic is not a profit-seeking corporation but a way of living in common that aims to ensure the dignity of its citizens, so it has the duty to offer assistance not as an act of compassion but in recognition of a right of citizenship. It must therefore take on the duty of assisting its citizens without making this help onerous and without assigning it to private individuals.[11]

FIVE

Republican Virtue

T O PROTECT LIBERTY, a republic must be able to rely on the civic virtue of its citizens, that is, on their willingness and capacity to serve the common good. Civic virtue is the foundation—or the spirit, to use Montesquieu's word—of republican government. Among some contemporary political theorists, however, the idea prevails that the civic virtue theorized by republican authors is impossible or dangerous or both. Impossible because citizens in our democracies are tied to group interests and have no motivation to serve the common good; dangerous because if in our multicultural societies citizens were to become more virtuous, they might also become more intolerant and more fanatic. Lastly, they claim, if we wished to let virtue reign, to make citizens virtuous, we would have to limit their liberties.[1]

The proximate origin of the idea that civic virtue is out of reach for modern citizens can be found in Montesquieu's *The*

Spirit of Laws. For Montesquieu, political virtue is the spirit of republican government, the dominant passion among its citizens if it is to survive and prosper. At the same time, he emphasizes that it is extremely difficult to instill in the hearts of citizens. It is necessary because the laws will become ineffective and the republic will dissolve if the citizens, out of greed or ambition, do not love the republic and its laws; it is extremely difficult because it is a form of renunciation, requiring citizens to moderate their desire for exclusive goods, that is, for goods such as wealth and honors whose value comes from being accessible to some but not all, at least not in the same quantities.[2]

To create virtuous citizens, Montesquieu wrote, one must teach them to guide their passions and desires toward common ends and goals: if they cannot pursue their private interests or wallow in the pleasures of private life, they will love the republic, just as monks love their order because the monastic rule deprives them of all that on which exclusive passions tend to fix. Citizens should live austerely and frugally: the more the republic succeeds in moderating private desires and passions, the more it becomes strong and united. In short, Montesquieu saw a threat to political virtue not only in greed and ambition but also in individual interests, and he believed that the ideal sites for political virtue were small republics that were frugal and austere.[3]

Montesquieu's writings on political virtue greatly influenced the political culture of the eighteenth century. Under the heading "*Patrie*" in the *Encyclopédie*, for instance, we read that political virtue is "love of the fatherland" ("*amour de la patrie*"), that is, a love of the laws and the good of the state that flourishes especially in democracies. A spirit of sacrifice is needed to place the common good above one's individual interest; this spiritual power gives strength even to the weakest, pushing them to accomplish great deeds for the public good (*"de grandes choses pour le bien public"*). And yet when modern people read about such virtuous citizens of antiquity, they consider them not paragons to be imitated but more likely fools to be derided.

Classical republican political writers, on the other hand, did not think of civic virtue as renunciation and sacrifice or as a way of life like the monastic one, which demands frugality and rejection of private goods. Nor did they consider political virtue a virtue for men cool to private passions, like Cato, or capable of crushing their own passions and affections, like Brutus. Coluccio Salutati, chancellor of the Florentine Republic from 1375 to 1406, for one, thought that political virtue required no sacrifice of one's passions and was in no way monastic. One need not imitate the marmoreal severity (*"marmorea quasi severitas"*) of Cato, he wrote to a friend, because even though he served the republic with great skill, Cato neglected his family ties.[4]

Following Cicero, the humanists repeat that while a philosopher in pursuit of wisdom is useful only to himself, a citizen working for the common good is useful to many other individuals. God is close to man even when man is immersed in the life of the city, or indeed anywhere that truth and virtue glimmer. As Matteo Palmieri explained in his book on civil life, written between 1435 and 1440, one need not seek perfect virtue, "the imaginary goodness of citizens such as have never been seen on earth," but rather study "the approved life of virtuous citizens with whom one has lived and may well live on earth" and pursue the virtue of civil men—earthly, imperfect, but pleasing to God.[5]

For Florentine republicans of the fifteenth century, civic virtue was not a sacrifice of private life but its very foundation, that which makes private life pleasant and secure. Exemplary in this regard is the dialogue between Giannozzo and Lionardo in Book III of *On the Family*, written by Leon Battista Alberti between 1433 and 1441:

> Like you, I would say that a good citizen loves tranquillity, but not so much his own tranquillity as that of other good men. He rejoices in his private leisure, but does not care less about that of his fellow citizens than about his own. He desires the unity, calm, peace, and tranquillity of his own house, but much more those of the country and of the republic. These good things, moreover, cannot be preserved if men of wealth or wisdom or nobility among the citizens seek more power than the other citizens, who are also free but less fortunate. Yet neither can these same republics be preserved if all the good men are solely content with their private leisure.

And later in the same text:

> Wise men say that good citizens should undertake to care for the republic and to toil at the tasks of their country, not shaken by the follies of men, in order to further the public peace and preserve the general good. Thus they also avoid giving a place of power to the

wicked, who through the indifference of the good and through their own dishonest wish soon pervert every plan and undermine both public and private well-being.[6]

Civic virtue can be onerous, especially for those who accept public duties. Those who manage the commonweal must be willing to face the animosity of "any and all evil and unjust citizens"; they must be capable of employing "extreme severity," and for good people severity is a burden. But if it is required, a good citizen cannot hang back; indeed, he must consider that "exterminating and extinguishing thieves and every sort of vicious individual, and every flame of unjust avarice," is "an exceedingly pious action." An act of piety, in other words, toward the fatherland, toward the republic: piety understood as a passion toward those who are dear to us—parents, relatives, sons and daughters, and compatriots. A virtuous citizen does not suppress passions with reason but allows one passion, civic charity, to prevail over the others and tries to balance civic virtue, and service to the republic, with private life.

For Florentine republicans, civic virtue was perfectly compatible with wealth. Suffice it to read the commentary written by Leonardo Bruni on the famous treatise on economics that is attributed to Aristotle but was probably written by Theophrastus. True, Bruni warns that if one begins to amass wealth beyond the needs of one's family, the thirst for money may become unquenchable ("*nullus est terminus divitiarum*"). But, he adds, wise men believe that wealth is not cause for criticism if it hurts no one. Indeed, riches can sustain such virtues as generosity and liberality, which are useful to the republic.

For Bruni, it is not true that virtue is sufficient unto itself and has no need of material goods, as the Stoics claim.[7] And the same idea can be found in the writings of Palmieri: for "gentlemen," he writes, riches are tools for the exercise of virtue, which without wealth remains "weak and incomplete."[8]

The basic outlines of this humanistic interpretation of civic virtue can be found as well in Machiavelli's work. Machiavelli did not share even remotely the ethic of sacrificing passions. He believed that civic life demands a certain decorum in the way one speaks, dresses, and behaves toward others; but he was tolerant of the variety of the world and of people's weaknesses. He pointed out that the laws can make men good, but he did not expect to make them perfect; he warned that to preserve a good republic, it was necessary to be inflexible with the arrogant and with those who wanted to be tyrants, but he did not think that citizens had to be saints. His conception of civic virtue had none of the marmoreal severity of Cato; it required not self-sacrifice but, rather, the expansion of certain passions at the expense of others.

When Machiavelli sets the ancient Romans as examples of virtue, he describes them not as a people who sacrificed their lives or private interests to the common good but as citizens who loved to live in freedom and therefore served liberty, because they wanted to enjoy their private lives in peace. A small portion among them, wrote Machiavelli, "desires to be free so as to command, but all the others, who are infinite, desire freedom so as to live secure."[9] The love of liberty, so strong in ancient peoples, grew from the fact that "all towns and provinces that live freely in every part . . . make very great profits. For larger peoples are seen there, because marriages

are freer and more desirable to men since each willingly pro-
creates those children he believes he can nourish. He does not
fear that his patrimony will be taken away, and he knows not
only that they are born free and not slaves, but that they can,
through their virtue, become princes."

In Machiavelli's view, uncorrupt citizens sacrifice nothing
but "in rivalry think of private *and* public advantages," and
because they do this, "both the one and the other come to
grow marvelously." Virtuous citizens love the security that living in freedom offers, they love the "sweetness of a free way of
life," and since they want to continue to enjoy that security
and that sweetness, they do their duty and obey the magistrates and laws when they must, and they know how to resist
and, when it becomes necessary, mobilize against those who
wish to destroy their free way of life.[10]

Like all humanists of the fifteenth century, Machiavelli
believed that thirst for glory was an important component in
civic virtue: the Roman people, he says, "loved the glory and
the common good of their fatherland." And he thought it was
important that this passion be felt by ordinary citizens and
especially by soldiers, because only "those who fight for their
own glory are good and faithful soldiers." And it is equally
important that when a republic is corrupt there be someone
who, out of love of fatherland and glory, has the strength to
redeem it: "And truly, if a prince seeks the glory of the world,
he ought to desire to possess a corrupt city—not to spoil it
entirely as did Caesar but to reorder it as did Romulus."[11] For
Machiavelli, glory dwelled in a city's squares and public
councils; love of glory by no means required a detachment
from private interests: the Roman people were fond of the

common good and the fatherland but also of their private and personal good.

One point on which Machiavelli differed from the humanists was the issue of poverty: did civic virtue require that citizens be poor? He saw wealth as a danger, not as a tool of civic virtue. He thought that the rich were dangerous to a republic because they tended toward arrogance and, by dispensing favors, could easily become the heads of factions that would place private interests over the common good. For that reason, he thought "well-ordered republics have to keep the public rich and their citizens poor."[12] (It is important to keep in mind that for Machiavelli poverty was merely the condition of having to continue working in order to live decently. Machiavelli considered himself poor after he lost his salary as a public official; he hadn't considered himself poor before so long as he had it. Even though he feared that his so-called poverty would prejudice others against him, his idea of poverty was not of a state defined by needs.)

Montesquieu and the theorists who came after him interpreted civic virtue as a virtue far more perfect and rigorous than that envisaged by the Italian civic humanists and by Renaissance writers. The latter had proclaimed a more human virtue, suited to individuals living in an earthly city who are neither gods nor saints and yet not beasts; a virtue that did not require them to sacrifice their passions and interests but tried to give liberty and private ties of affection a secure political foundation and moral enrichment; a virtue that accepted variety in ways of living because that's how the world is and it's fine that it is. It is quite understandable that a writer in eighteenth-century France, drawing on classical sources, should view civic virtue in a distant, more ideal and luminous way, so luminous as to seem impossible. But those who actually lived in a republic thought of a less severe quality, lighter and, by that very token, plausible.

This is a civic virtue for men and women who wish to live in dignity, and since they know it is impossible to live in dignity when the community is corrupt, they do everything they can, whenever they can, to serve the common liberty: they do their jobs in good conscience, without taking illicit advantage and without profiting from others' need or vulnerability; members of their family respect each other, so that their homes resemble little republics more than they do monarchies or a collection of strangers held together by mere self-interest or by television; they perform their civic duties, but they are not docile; they can mobilize to prevent the passage of an unjust law or to push their leaders to deal with problems in the common interest; they are active in associations of various sorts—professional, athletic, cultural, political, or religious; they take an interest in national and international politics; they want to understand, and they do not want to be guided or indoctrinated; they want to know, discuss, and reflect on the history of their nation.

For some, the chief motivation for commitment comes from a moral sense, more precisely, from indignation at abuse, discrimination, corruption, arrogance, or vulgarity; for others, from an aesthetic desire for decency and decorum; still others are driven by specific concerns—about safe streets, pleasant parks, well-kept squares, respected monuments, good schools and hospitals; or people become engaged because they want to gain repute and they aspire to attain public honor, sit at the

chairman's table, give speeches, stand in the front row at cere-
monies. In many cases these motives work together, reinforcing each other.

This type of civic virtue is neither impossible nor dangerous, and it is as republican as any other. Each of us can think
of people who answer to this description of a citizen with a
sense of civic responsibility, and we can say that they have only
brought good to their community and to themselves. Problems
arise when this type of civic culture is suffocated by other ways
of living, especially by a culture of arrogance and servility. If
those who govern and those who pass laws would reward more
often those who deserve it and who do good for the republic,
rather than heaping honors on the slick and the sly, civic culture would grow in strength.

Is it too late? I think the best answer to this question was
offered by Tocqueville:

> No laws can bring back life to fading beliefs, but laws
> can make men care for the fate of their countries. It
> depends on the laws to awaken and direct that vague
> instinct of patriotism which never leaves the human
> heart, and by linking it to everyday thoughts, passions,
> and habits, to make it a conscious and durable senti-
> ment. And one should never say that it is too late to
> attempt that; nations do not grow old as men do. Each
> fresh generation is new material for the lawgiver to
> mold.[13]

Republican Patriotism

T HE PROBLEM OF CIVIC VIRTUE, that is, the citizens' interest in the public good, brings us to the issue of patriotism. For centuries, republican political writers have claimed that the chief passion that gives power to civic virtue is love of the fatherland; often they have considered the two concepts identical. Given the importance of the problem, it is no surprise that republican political literature is so rich in references to and treatments of patriotism. But it is a surprise that in modern times most neo-republican theorists have failed to give it the attention it deserves. The lack is glaring, and I shall try to remedy it.

In classical republicanism, love of country is, to be precise, a charitable love of the republic (*caritas reipublicae*) and of one's fellow citizens (*caritas civium*). The concept of *caritas* passes from the Roman sources to the works of the scholastic political writers of the Middle Ages who supported self-government of local communes. Ptolemy of Lucca, for one, wrote that "love of the fatherland grows from the root of charity, which places not private goods above common goods but, rather, common goods above private goods."

Even when it respects the principles of justice and reason and can therefore be called "rational love," love of the fatherland is a specific affection for a specific republic and its citizens. It is found especially among citizens of free republics, who share many important things—laws, liberty, public councils, public squares, friends and enemies, memories of victories and defeats, hopes and fears. It presupposes civil and political equality, and it translates into acts of service (*officium*) and care (*cultus*) for the common good. Lastly, *caritas reipublicae* (literally, charity toward the commonweal) invigorates the soul, giving citizens the strength to perform their civic duties and rulers the courage to meet the often onerous obligations that defense of the common liberty demands.

In the language of patriotism which scholastic political authors used in their writings and sermons, the Roman concept of *caritas* lived once again, now accompanied by Christian themes. The marriage of these two traditions was a distinctive characteristic of Florentine patriotism of the fourteenth and fifteenth centuries, though that patriotism was fiercely anticlerical, as is shown by the saying "to love one's fatherland more than one's soul," which any priest would find heretical. Yet it was also profoundly Christian. Unless we are aware of this intellectual context, we cannot understand the meaning of a passage in Machiavelli's *Discourses* in which, after a quite radical attack on Christian religion and education, he notes that Christianity, if properly interpreted, "permits us the exaltation and defense of the fatherland . . . [I]t wishes us to love and honor it and to prepare ourselves to be such that we can defend it."[1] While the political writings of the scholastics were not among his favorite reading and he rarely went to church, even Machiavelli recognized the existence of a Christian patriotism in which Roman themes lived on.

The language of patriotism was significant in the projects of political reform theorized, and at times attempted, in the Italian states of the late sixteenth and seventeenth centuries. The central theme, then, both in states governed by Italian princes and in those controlled by foreign powers, was equality, understood as "a principle of solidarity based on membership in a community and on common interest." Equality of the citizens, the historian Rosario Villari has explained,

> did not exclude juridical disparities and a certain degree of inequality of political rights. Nor did it amount to respect for the law, pure and simple. It included a call for a *governo largo*, or "broad government," as a condition whereby it would be possible to establish the stable authority of the law and to prevent arbitrary rule, anarchy, and tyranny. The essential objective . . . was to consolidate the civil bond linking all members of the community, the subordination of one and all, great and small, each at his own level of social and political power, to the general interest.[2]

In the eighteenth century, the language of republican patriotism took on a more distinctly political significance, though entirely consistent with the classical conceptions of *caritas reipublicae* and *caritas civium*. "*Patrie*," we read in the *Encyclopédie*, for instance, means not the place in which we were born, as is the common understanding, but, rather, a "free state" ("*état libre*") of which we are members and whose laws protect "our liberty and our happiness" ("*nos libertés et notre bonheur*"). The political writers of the Enlightenment used the word "fatherland" synonymously with "republic," because they believed that the true fatherland could only be a free republic. This identification was not merely polemical: it summarized the idea that under the yoke of a despot, citizens are without protection and cannot participate in public life; they might as well be outsiders, and they therefore have no fatherland. Following Montesquieu, the author of the entry in the *Encyclopédie* wrote: "Those who live under oriental despotism, where there is no law but the will of the sovereign, no other maxim than the adoration of his caprices, no other principles of government than terror, where no fortune is safe, no head lies easy—those people have no *patrie*, and they do not even know the word, which is the very expression of happiness."[3]

To these political writers of the eighteenth century, love of the fatherland was not a natural sentiment but an artificial feeling to be fostered by laws or, better yet, by good government and participation in public life. "Let our country, then," wrote Rousseau in his *Economie politique*, "show itself the common mother of her citizens; let the advantages they enjoy in their country endear it to them; let the government leave them enough share in the public administration to make them feel they are at home; and let the laws be in their eyes only the guarantees of the common liberty."[4]

With his customary mastery, Rousseau linked the father-land with liberty and virtue: "There can be no patriotism without liberty, no liberty without virtue, no virtue without citizens." In his best-sellers *Emile* and *La Nouvelle Héloïse*, he reiterated the distinction between *pays* and *patrie*: without liberty and without true citizens one can speak not of a father-land but only of a country.[5] The foundations of the fatherland lie in the relationship between the citizens and the state and a way of life in keeping with republican institutions: "It is nei-ther walls nor men who make the fatherland: it is laws, cus-toms, habits, government, and the way of life that ensues therefrom. The fatherland lies in the relations between the state and its members; when these relations change or fail, the fatherland ceases to exist."[6]

Just a few years later, Gaetano Filangieri summarized in his *Science of Legislation* the significance of republican patriot-ism: "Let us not misuse the sacred name of *love of country* to indicate that affection for the soil of the fatherland which is an appendix of the very evils of civil unions and which can be found both in the most corrupt and in the most perfect soci-eties." True *love of country*, he claimed, is an artificial passion: "It can be dominant and unknown; it can have absolutely no vigor in one people and be omnipotent in another. The wisdom of the law and of government introduces it, establishes it, expands it, and invigorates it; the defects of both weaken it, exclude it, and proscribe it."[7]

The idea that good government and participation in public life are at the root of true patriotism naturally develops into the idea that true patriotism is born and flourishes in local self-government. One of the first theorists of local self-government as the root of civil patriotism was Giandomenico Romagnosi: "True patriotism is found in the city hall. The spring—dependable, active, real, and permanent—of true and certain patriotism is in the city hall, and I dare say it can be found there and there only. Let me add: there alone is the foundation for security in everything and the political ordering of a civil state."[8] The same concept reemerges in the pages of *Democracy in America* where Tocqueville describes the patriotism he finds in the townships of New England: "It is important to appreciate that, in general, men's affections are drawn only in directions where power exists. Patriotism does not long prevail in a conquered country. The New Englander is attached to his township not so much because he was born there as because he sees the township as a free, strong corporation of which he is part and which is worth the trouble of trying to direct."[9]

When Carlo Cattaneo wrote, in 1864, that "the communes are the nation; they are the nation in the most intimate nursery of its liberty," he captured in a marvelous phrase, rich in profundity and expressive power, a long republican tradition about patriotism.[10] Giuseppe Mazzini did the same, but in a different direction, at once more unitary and more democratic. He emphasized that the true fatherland ensures to all citizens not only civil and political rights but also the right to work and to education:

> The fatherland is not a territory; the territory is nothing but the foundation. The fatherland is an idea built on that foundation; it is the thought of love, the sense of communion that binds all the children of that territory into one. As long as one of your brothers is not repre-

sented by a vote in the development of national life, as
long as one languishes uneducated among the edu-
cated, as long as a single person who is ready and willing to work lies idle, in poverty, due to lack of a job, you
will not have the fatherland that you should have, the
fatherland of all, the fatherland for all.[11]

Mazzini also says that the fatherland is a common house,
where we live with people we understand and hold dear because we feel they are like us and close to us. But it is a house
that stands alongside other houses of equal worth. When we
are in our own house, we must perform our duties as citizens;
when we are in the houses of others, we must perform our
duties toward humanity. To defend liberty is the supreme duty
of each one of us, even if the people being oppressed are in a
foreign land. Our moral obligations toward humanity come
before our obligations toward our fatherland. Before being citizens of a particular fatherland, we are human beings, and this
means that national barriers cannot be a pretext for moral
deafness. The voices of suffering people must be heard wherever they are raised. However great the differences among cultures, love of liberty makes translation possible.[12]

So for Mazzini there is no need to renounce patriotism in
order to support the cause of humanity. On the contrary, that
cause can be supported most effectively by building one's
homeland first of all. As individuals, we can do very little to
help those who do not belong to our nation. At the most we
can offer charitable gestures or exchange occasional favors,
like good neighbors, but we cannot work together on common
enterprises. There has to be a mediating between an individual

and humanity at large; this is what nations are, and the free, republican fatherlands built in them. These are the God-given means by which to carry out the plan for humanity's development. We must therefore begin with the fatherland; we cannot even dream of being able to help humanity without first helping our country.[13]

The considerations set forth thus far and the texts I have quoted—I could easily add others—clarify the difference between republican patriotism and nationalism. Classical political writers were quite clear on this point: the political and cultural values of the fatherland differ from the nonpolitical values of the nation. They used two different terms to describe them: *patria* and *natio*. Both *patria* and *natio* establish bonds among individuals, but the bonds of the *patria*, or *res publica*, are stronger and nobler than the bonds of the *natio*, as Cicero wrote.[14]

The ancient distinction is still valid. Theorists of republican patriotism considered that the republic's political institutions, and the way of life based on them, had the highest political value; nationalists, on the other hand, put the people's cultural or ethnic or religious identity in the forefront. The former considered the only true fatherland a free republic; for the latter, a fatherland exists wherever a people has preserved its cultural identity.

A further distinction concerns the interpretation of love of country. For republicans, as I have pointed out, love of country was an artificial feeling that required constant stoking and nourishment by political means, first and foremost good government and participation in public life. For nationalists, in contrast, love of country was a natural emotion which, to thrive and grow strong, had to be protected from contamination and cultural assimilation. This difference obviously derives from the former considering the republic as a political institution, and the latter considering the nation as produced by nature, or God.

Yet a republic is not a purely political institution, distinct from a nation understood as a cultural reality. The republic, being a political order and a way of life, is a culture. Machiavelli spoke of *living* free; others defined the republic as "a certain life of the city."[15] Thus republican patriotism has a cultural significance: it is a political passion based on the experience of republican equality and love of a certain culture, although it does not assign great value to the matter of being born in a given territory, belonging to the same ethnic group, speaking the same language, having the same customs, or worshipping the same gods or god. Those who claim that republican patriotism cannot be a valid response to the problems of social and political cohesion in contemporary societies because it is a purely political credo are off the mark: republican patriotism is by no means a purely political credo.

Nor is the idea of nation or the principle of nationality opposed to republican patriotism. Consider the definition of the principle of nationality that John Stuart Mill developed in his *System of Logic*:

We need scarcely say that we do not mean nationality, in the vulgar sense of the term; a senseless antipathy to foreigners; indifference to the general welfare of the human race, or an unjust preference of the supposed interests of our own country; a cherishing of bad peculiarities because they are national, or a refusal to adopt what has been found good by other countries. We mean a principle of sympathy, not of hostility; of union, not of separation. We mean a feeling of common interest among those who live under the same government, and are contained within the same natural or historical boundaries. We mean, that one part of the community do not consider themselves as foreigners with regard to another part; that they set a value on their connection—feel that they are one people, that their lot is cast together, that evil to any of their fellow-countrymen is evil to themselves, and do not desire selfishly to free themselves from their share of any common inconvenience by severing the connection.[16]

This conception of the nation became an integral part of republican patriotism in the nineteenth and twentieth centuries, as Massimo Salvadori has explained. The distinctive feature of republican patriotism, he writes, is

the sense of the value of liberty as a good of all and for all; fidelity and loyalty toward institutions deriving from equal participation; a system of rights that bases citizenship in a republic on respect for the individual on the one hand and for groups on the other, that is, on the implementation and defense of a pluralism that may be competitive but need not become mutually destructive; a political system that derives from a common pact, demands a tireless defense of the established rules in order to define relations between those who govern and those who are governed, between the state and civil society; a civic conscience nourished by love of the fatherland which, in the garb of virtue, requires one to fight against the degeneration of power and the evil of corruption; a way of experiencing politics that is manifest on the public stage and that rejects the *arcana imperii*; a public ethics that demands loyalty to public institutions above and beyond any private loyalties; a spirit that conceives of the fatherland as an ideal, not a physical, place, and therefore considers territoriality as implementing the universal values of humanity in a specific space.[17]

Perhaps the most precise meaning of republican patriotism was expressed, in words that are especially touching because of the intentional absence of rhetoric, by Giacomo Ulivi, in one of his last letters before being executed in 1944, at the age of nineteen, by a fascist firing squad:

Believe me, the "public good" is ourselves; what ties us to it is not a cliché, a big empty word like "patriotism" or our love for a mother who calls upon us, in chains and in tears . . . If we think about it, our interests and the interests of the "public good" in short wind up being the same thing. Precisely for this reason, we need to take direct, personal care of it, and consider it our most delicate and important task. Because all our other tasks, the conditions for all our other tasks, depend on this one.[18]

Republican patriotism, then, differs from both ethnic and civic nationalism. In contrast with the former, it recognizes no political or moral value in the unity and ethnic homogeneity of a people, while it does recognize the moral and political importance of values of citizenship, which are entirely incompatible with any form of ethnocentrism. In contrast with the latter, it proclaims allegiance not to culturally and historically neutral political principles but to the laws, constitutions, and ways of life of specific republics, each with its own history and culture.

Civic virtue and the culture of republican citizenship do not bloom on the branch of cultural or ethnic or religious homogeneity. People who boast an elevated degree of homogeneity in ethnic, cultural, or religious terms are often distinguished more by intolerance and bigotry than by their civic sense. Only true republican politics can bring about a rebirth of civic culture in modern democratic societies without the help of cultural or ethnic homogeneity.

Civic virtue can also easily do without religion, though classical republicans thought differently. Machiavelli, for example, accused the church of having put the greatest stock "in humility, abjectness, and contempt of things human," of having taught that strength consists in being capable "more of suffering than of doing something strong," and therefore of having made the "world weak" and thus easy prey for "criminal men." All the same, he believed that religion, especially fear of God, was essential "to commanding armies, animating the plebs, keeping men good, bringing shame to the wicked." He even wrote that divine worship and fear of God were especially necessary in republics: "As the observance of the divine cult is the cause of the greatness of republics, so disdain for it is the cause of their ruin. For where the fear of God fails, it must be either that the kingdom comes to ruin or that it is sustained by the fear of a prince, which supplies the defects of religion."[19]

Three centuries later, analyzing the institutions and customs of the first great republic of the modern world, Tocqueville praised the United States' sharp separation of church and state but wrote that what counted most in American society was not that all citizens profess a true religion but that they profess some religion. America, he said, where religion had great power over people, was "the most enlightened and free" nation on earth. It was political liberty itself that made religion necessary: "For my part, I doubt whether man can support complete religious independence and entire political liberty at the same time. I am led to think that if he has no faith he must obey, and if he is free he must believe."[20]

Machiavelli and Tocqueville, two very different writers, follow different paths to reach the same conclusion: republics have special need of religion to orient their citizens in their moral lives and to instill in them a sense of duty that will lead them to respect the laws and perform their civic obligations. Machiavelli's argument singles out an important truth: religious belief and the fear of God penetrate the hearts of individuals and guide their actions; political authority and laws, with their rewards and sanctions, fail to do this, merely conditioning actions without influencing motivations except very minimally. Unless another force can quicken internal motivations into action, we must accept the necessity of religion.

But such a force does exist: patriotism. Tocqueville wrote that patriotism "never leaves the human heart" and can become, through law, a lasting and conscious feeling linked to one's thoughts, passions, and daily customs. Patriotism, then, shares with religion the ability to enter into the heart and move people to action in a lasting manner. As Tocqueville put it:

"Patriotism and religion are the only things in the world which will make the whole body of citizens go persistently forward toward the same goal."[21]

A republic that could count on religion, especially the Christian religion, and on republican patriotism would be, then, as good and united as one could hope. But one need not aspire to such perfection. A republic of patriotic and religious citizens is unlikely to be a tolerant one. Civic patriotism seasoned by a sense of proportion and a healthy dose of irony and doubt would be more than sufficient. Wherever this kind of patriotism already exists, I would not be too concerned about its lacking a religious spirit, which after all concerns an aspect of human life that should be none of the state's business and that should be pursued solely through spiritual means and left entirely to the faithful. What is certain, in any case, is that a republic cannot do without both patriotism and religion; one cannot expect personal interest or adherence to universal principles of liberty to be enough to foster civil responsibility. Personal interests alone will not move anyone to uphold the public good, and while universal principles may win the endorsement of reason, they rarely drive one to take action. One must choose, and I believe that the wisest choice would be civil patriotism.

In response to Tocqueville's view that it is existentially impossible to live free without the support of the certainties of religion, I believe we may say that political liberty is more in need of the sense of doubt proper to the secular soul than the certainties of religious faith. It needs people who have strong views about political and moral values but with equal passion believe in and experience these values not as absolute truths but as possible choices alongside other possible choices. The republican ethic finds meaning and beauty as much in public life and in a commitment to build and preserve civic life as in private life and in meditation and reflection. It does not try to reduce the individual to the citizen or private life to public life, inner life to active life. It sees the various dimensions of life as completing one another. It indicates a way to give individual life a meaning that does not end with death, a mode of actions and speech that lives on after us in the memories of others.

The republican ethic can therefore coexist with religious belief, but it has no need of it in facing the weighty moral choices that liberty allows and demands. It can and must remain rigorously secular. Nowadays being secular means being committed to excluding religious doctrines, and the institutions that support and proclaim them, from all operations of the public good, or commonweal. Secularism is opposed first of all to confessionalism and integralism, doctrines that say a state's political institutions and laws may impose on all—believers and nonbelievers alike—the religious principles of an established religion. Second, secularism is opposed to clericalism, the citizens' routine obedience (sadly quite common in Italian politics, for example) to directives of the church and ecclesiastical hierarchy on social and political questions. Secularism is also a conception of culture and civil life that in general detests dogmatism, as well as all simplistic and sweeping solutions to social problems. One proof of this can be seen in recent European history, during which secular political movements and parties were hostile to communist totalitarianism, which they condemned, significantly, for being "the other church."

Precisely because they reject the certitude of dogmas, secular politics and republics have a great need of memory and commemoration. Memory is a powerful means for encouraging civic virtue. The democratic republics that most assiduously defend the separation of church and state—the United States and France—are also those that are especially committed to celebrating their own history. When we commemorate a long-ago episode of resistance to tyranny or a struggle for liberty; when we hark back to a painful page of our shared history; when we speak of martyrs, of the men or women who made contributions to the republic, who established an association or founded a league, we can arouse in the hearts of the participants a sense of moral obligation to carry on the work. The past can become a resource for the civic education of new generations.

People may think that commemorations, especially republican ones, are manifestations of a dusty patriotism, relics of bygone times, no longer of value in the days of market globalization and exploding scientific knowledge. But a people that cannot give meaning, value, and beauty to its own history is unlikely to acquire that dignity which is an indispensable premise of civic culture. Just as a person with low self-esteem becomes either servile or arrogant, a people with no national pride cannot but be a people of servants or clients, easily transformed into cruel oppressors of the weak. We have no need of pompous national pride, constructed out of cowardly or pathetic lies about the greatness of the fatherland and our ancestors. Such nationalistic hubris is offensive to anyone who objects to being treated like an infant. But we need to rediscover in our own national histories the important experiences of liberty, however brief or snuffed out in military defeat. For Italians, there is the Roman Republic of 1849 and the Neapolitan Republic of 1799: these can make us feel like inheritors of a history with a dignity that imposes on us the moral obligation to make our country a genuine civil community.

To give meaning and value to our history, we must understand it, feel it, and think about it carefully. If we are to commemorate with the right words and the proper tone of voice, then we must understand the meaning of the republican ideal and what it meant to those who made the supreme sacrifice in order to put it into practice. The problem is that the forces currently dominating the intellectual and political landscape all too often know nothing about, or look with arrogance or scorn upon, the historical memories, the myths, and the martyrs of the republican experience. If the remaining strength of our republican tradition were to dwindle away, this cultural and moral heritage would in a few years be buried and forgotten, and with it we would lose one of the most precious resources for the rebirth of a civil conscience. In Italy, for example, republicans can be proud of having kept alive the tradition of commemorating the Roman Republic, but even those who are not republicans should not be condescending about this, but be grateful to them.

I believe that republicanism has the historical and moral resources to revive or indeed engender civic enthusiasm, without a revelation of faith and without a dogmatic belief in history or in a leader. Either we shall find a way to reinforce republican politics and culture, or we shall have to resign ourselves to living in nations whose governments are controlled by the cunning and the arrogant.

Now, at the dawn of the new century, we seem to be witnessing a moral and political retreat on the part of the kind of open-minded political and secular forces I have been recommending. "It is a common belief even among the secular," Gian Enrico Rusconi has written, "that the church and church religion are the privileged repositories of the values needed for civil coexistence." When television sets show the head of the Roman Catholic church together with the world's highest secular political figure, the president of the United States, and when we hear the pope speak out against social injustice, the death penalty, and racism, it is difficult not to see the pope as standard-bearer of values and Bill Clinton as the symbol of a politics that no longer has the strength of ideals.

It is my impression that it has become a common belief that churches, synagogues, and mosques are the guardians of the moral values of personal dignity, liberty, and social justice, while secular forces are concerned with power and indeed hold power: churches carry on persuasive debates over values and the meaning of life, practice solidarity, organize volunteer activities; in contrast, secular forces speak of market constraints, the global economy, a united Europe, or electoral reforms that are of little interest to voters. If things continue like this, secular politics has no future, because any power, including ecclesiastical power, that establishes its own values and affirms itself as a moral guide expects to be a political guide as well—and rightly so. It can therefore impose conditions on its competitors.

I believe, all the same, that a rebirth of secular culture and politics is possible, that secular politics can once again play a major role. But this will happen only if it manages to become a form of politics inspired by strong moral ideals and if it can insist on the need for social justice. Secular politics must above all respect the principle of consistency between words and deeds. As Norberto Bobbio wrote in the years after World War II, the secular principle "is consistency; its norm is sincerity."[22] Those who experience politics with the faith of a believer (or fanatic) or with the cynicism of a deal maker can tolerate what we call jesuitical evasiveness, indeed, will accept it and seek it out. But citizens who are involved in politics because they want to establish legitimate ideals and interests will not tolerate it, and we know that when secular parties become stingy and corrupt, they stray far from politics.

The most daunting problem that republican politics faces remains this issue of causing, encouraging, and diffusing the rebirth of a civic patriotism. Since reinforcing the cultural, moral, or religious unity of a people is not only incompatible with the principle of liberty but also counterproductive, what remains are the sterling policies suggested countless times by political writers in the past. The first and most important element is justice. If we want citizens to love their republic and its laws, then the republic and its laws must equally protect all of them, without offering privileges to the powerful or discriminating against the weak. This means that the republic must punish always and only in accordance with the laws, in full respect of the rights of the accused and in full respect of the law; it must punish large and small crimes with equal firmness: the crime of the powerful individual and the crime of the small tyrant who afflicts the weak.

The principle of absolute respect for the rule of law must apply especially to public officials and politicians when they have committed crimes against human rights and against the common good, under the protection of a flag or a uniform, and when they have taken up arms to suppress liberty. Often the tendency is to forgive such people and to assume they will turn over a new leaf, rather than punishing them in accordance with the law, remembering, and causing others to remember. Those who tell us to forgive and forget maintain that it is impossible to punish properly (because the guilty are too many or too powerful), or that it is nobler to pardon them, or that we must be able to continue to live together as a people.

Republican wisdom teaches, instead, that to preserve a civil way of life, and a political order in which the laws are respected, the greatest severity is required in the punishment of citizens who are found guilty of serious crimes, especially when these are important, well-known, powerful citizens. Machiavelli called such punishments "memorable executions" and wrote that they "made men draw back toward the mark whenever one of them arose; and when they began to be more rare, they also began to give more space to men to corrupt themselves." From one execution to the next, he wrote, no more than ten years should pass, "for when this time is past, men begin to vary in their customs and to transgress the laws. Unless something arises by which punishment is brought back to their memory and fear is renewed in their spirits, soon so many delinquents join together that they can no longer be punished without danger."[23]

Republican politics neither calls for nor justifies revenge, even for the most atrocious crimes. Revenge may sometimes quench a thirst, as was the case with a survivor of the death camps who killed with his own hands the doctor who had sent his family members to the gas chamber. When it was pointed out to him that his deed had done nothing to bring his dead relatives back to life, he answered that his vengeance "brought *me* back to life."[24] But revenge almost never heals wounds, it does nothing to resolve trauma, and it only triggers an unstoppable chain reaction of reprisals.

Matters are different when it comes to the punishment of guilty parties inflicted by public or supranational institutions acting with full respect of judicial limits. Such public punishment must uphold the principle of equal dignity of all persons, and it must correct the false message—implicit in mass crimes and in ordinary crimes—that the victims are of less value than the criminals. We must reestablish the human value of the victims by inflicting a public defeat on the criminals.

Public pardons that are translated into amnesties or condonations corrode the republic, just as a vendetta would do, but for the opposite reasons. A pardon can be extended by a victim, but that in no way eliminates the judicial requirement of justice and punishment. When states arrogate to themselves the right to pardon and to proclaim amnesties, they institutionalize forgetfulness and sacrifice the requirement of justice in favor of the urge to forget and move on. Thus amnesties and condonations are not instances of genuine pardons, the exclusive prerogative of the victim, but ways of publicly ignoring the wrong that has been committed. I cannot see a public pardon as an act of charity, endowed with moral dignity, though certainly there is enormous dignity in a victim's choosing to extend a pardon. True charity, love for the public good and for the liberty and dignity of all citizens, translates into a relentless defense of law.

The same requirement of justice and equality that must guide the administration of sentences should be present in the distribution of public prizes and honors. The clearest and most eloquent words on this subject are Machiavelli's: "A free way of life proffers honors and rewards through certain honest and determinate causes, and outside these it neither rewards nor honors anyone." He meant to emphasize that to remain faithful to its own principles, a republic should distribute prizes and honors according to norms designed to protect the public good. Hence, neither wealth nor friendship nor membership in a faction—only merit and the capacity to serve the common good—may open the doors to public honors, to prestigious offices and jobs.

A republican politics that rewards those who wish to serve the public good, and have the skill and training to do so, will produce and reproduce a high-level ruling elite; it can engender a virtuous social hierarchy that will stimulate neither envy nor resentment (save among the wretched and corrupt); and it fosters healthy competition to excel in the right way. The politics of rewards and recognition that prevails in all too many countries today has, instead, largely been a politics of patronage—that is, the distribution of jobs, profits, and privileges according to the willingness of a citizen to be loyal to a person or faction. This politics of patronage creates a corrupt and incompetent elite, it undermines the moral soul of the republic, and it encourages unhealthy competition. A court of law in Milan that not long ago declared exempt from punishment some politicians who had distributed civil-service jobs in the hospitals of Lombardy in accordance with the party affiliations of the job seekers did serious harm to the Italian republic. That verdict, in fact, taught us two things that are particularly repugnant to a civil conscience: that by kowtowing to a powerful person one can get a job, and that rewarding one's friends rather than someone of merit is not illicit.

Civil patriotism is encouraged by justice, but also by participation in civic self-rule. As republican political writers have emphasized over and over, citizens who participate in communal self-government, attend debates, express opinions in public councils, elect representatives and monitor their work—such citizens feel the public good to be something that is theirs, and they develop toward it an attachment similar to what they feel toward their own property.

Of course, the institutions of the republic are public, and they don't belong to any single individual or group exclusively. When they become private, we say that a republic is corrupt or, to use the classical language, no longer a *res publica*. Being public, they don't arouse an interest comparable to that felt toward property we own exclusively, but participation can correct this state of affairs, bringing the republic closer and making people feel it is theirs and dear to them.

Citizens take participation seriously only when they have a chance to make a difference and when the problems discussed affect their interests directly, as Tocqueville noted in connection with town meetings in New England. If we wish to revive political participation and civic spirit, then we should give townships and cities the power to make important decisions for the life of the collectivity. The greater the power of local institutions, the greater attraction they will have to citizens concerned with their own interests and eager to distinguish themselves, to prompt admiration, to exert influence and authority. There is nothing wrong with this. Quite the contrary, the best republican politics is, precisely, a politics that can speak to self-interest in the best sense and to the just ambition to distinguish oneself.

Men and women learn citizenship when they go to union meetings, join sports groups, attend city council hearings, participate in church activities, or become members of a political party: all these practices occur in places and contexts that are culturally dense, specific, meaningful. Citizenship is dressed in many different colors, nourished by different memories, identified with the words of different prophets, kept alive by, among other things, festivities that belong to the historical experience of different cultural groups. The kind of commonality we should aim at is therefore a culture of citizenship that is cultivated not by means of universal political principles applied to specific cultures, not by dispersing particular cultures throughout a common universal political frame, not by strengthening the cultural homogeneity of different groups, but by encouraging many civic traditions within different groups.

A politics designed to expand the boundaries of liberty and to enhance citizenship must be a politics of social justice designed to grant all citizens the rights that permit them to have dignified lives, a politics of civil society designed to strengthen a rich and diverse net of associations: unions, cultural associations, religious communities, ecological groups, sports clubs, local communities, neighborhoods, and so on. It is better to have more of them than fewer. Dissociated individuals who live solely within the sphere of family and work, when they do work, are inclined to heed nationalist or religious demagogues.

Democratic institutions today are suffering a serious malaise, a lack of passion, commitment, or loyalty that affects different democratic countries differently but affects them all. American scholars speak of a collapse of civic engagement; European political scientists speak of a passionless Europe. Passion, commitment, and loyalty seem to have forsaken democracy and to have followed nationalistic and religious demagogues. Republicanism should propose itself in democratic multicultural countries as a new political vision of a civic ethos that reconnects the words "liberty" and "responsibility." To accomplish this, republicanism must keep its distinctive intellectual and political identity and remain faithful to its founding principles.

Bibliography

Among the classic works, Aristotle's *Politics* deserves special mention, even if Aristotle was not, properly speaking, a republican writer, for it contains the doctrine of the *politeia*, understood as a political constitution that is legitimate in general terms (inasmuch as it is based on the common good and the rule of law); from this the Roman idea of *res publica* derived. For the theory of forms of government, especially the idea of the cycle of governments and of mixed government, the basic text is Book VI of Polybius's *Histories*. Another basic text is the gallery of examples of republican virtue offered in Plutarch's *Lives*.

The classical theory of the *res publica* is found in the works of Roman political authors and historians written when the *res publica* was nothing more than a memory, especially Cicero's *De re publica* and *De officiis*. Aside from the works of Cicero, Livy's *Histories* is essential, as are the works of Sallust. To understand the persistence of republican ideals in Rome's imperial era, one should read Tacitus, *Annales*, vol. 2, *Agricola and Germany* (Oxford: Oxford University Press, 1999).

The brief but important experience of Italy's free communes produced a republican political literature primarily of reflections on the idea of *civitas* and on the obligations and virtues of the highest office in the communal government. Examples of this literature are the anonymous

Bibliography

Oculus pastoralis, ed. Dora Franceschi, Memorie dell'Accademia delle Scienze di Torino, ser. 4, no. 11 (1966): 3–70; Orfino da Lodi, *De regimine et sapientia potestatis*, ed. A. Ceruti, *Miscellanea di Storia Italiana* 7 (1869): 33–94; Giovanni da Viterbo, *Liber de regimine civitatum*, ed. G. Salvemini, in *Bibliotheca juridica medii aevi*, vol. 3 (Bologna, 1901), 215–80; Brunetto Latini, *Li livres dou Trésor*, ed. Francis J. Carmody (Berkeley: University of California Press, 1948; reprint, Geneva: Slatkine, 1975). Also of fundamental importance are the works of fourteenth- and fifteenth-century Italian jurists who developed the juridical definition of a free city, and also Marsilio of Padua's *Defensor pacis*, or *In Defense of Peace*. For the idea of republican government as the most efficacious means for attaining the fullest form of civil and political life, see *De regimine principum*, in *Divi Thomae Aquinatis opuscula philosophiae*, ed. Raimondo Spiazzi (Turin: Marietti, 1954), especially Book IV, written by Ptolemy of Lucca.

Themes of republican liberty and the virtues of citizens and laws lie at the center of the political theory of Florence's civic humanists. One of the first modern scholars to explore this area was Hans Baron, whose studies on the subject have been collected in two volumes, *In Search of Florentine Civic Humanism* (Princeton, N.J.: Princeton University Press, 1988). The most significant works of this important early period of republican political thought are those of Coluccio Salutati, *Invectiva in Antonium Luschum Vicentinum*, in *Prosatori latini del Quattrocento*, ed. Eugenio Garin (Milan and Naples: Ricciardi, 1952), and *Il trattato "De tyranno" e lettere scelte*, ed. Francesco Ercole (Bologna: Zanichelli, 1942); Leonardo Bruni, *Panegirico della città di Firenze*, facing Italian text by Frate Lazaro da Padova, intro. by Giuseppe de Toffol (Florence: La Nuova Italia, 1974); Alamanno Rinuccini, *Lettere e orazioni*, ed. Vito Giustiniani (Florence: Olschki, 1953), and "Dialogus de Libertate," in *Atti e Memorie dell'Accademia Toscana di Scienze e Lettere La Colombaria* 21 (1956): 265–303. This last publication develops a complete republican interpretation of the relationship between political liberty and civic virtue.

The work that best summarizes the republicanism of the fifteenth-century Florentine humanists is still Matteo Palmieri, *Vita civile*, ed. Gino Belloni (Florence: Olschki, 1981). Also of considerable importance are the sermons of Savonarola, above all his *Trattato circa el reggi-*

mento e governo della città di Firenze, in *Prediche sopra Aggeo*, ed. Luigi Firpo (Rome: Belardetti, 1965), which contains the fundamental principles of the constitutional reform of the republic of 1494–1512 that he implemented. And of course one must consult Thomas More's *Utopia*, perhaps the most significant text of civil humanism in northern Europe.

The riper fruit of republican political thought came to light, as is so often the case, when the republics were reaching their end in Italy. In the early sixteenth century, works were written that laid the foundations of modern republicanism, first and foremost those of Niccolò Machiavelli, especially his *Discourses on Livy*, trans. Harvey C. Mansfield and Nathan Tarcov (Chicago: University of Chicago Press, 1996). Also fundamental were the works of Francesco Guicciardini, notably his *Dialogue on the Government of Florence* (Cambridge, U.K.: Cambridge University Press, 1994); Donato Giannotti, in particular *Della repubblica fiorentina* and *Della repubblica de Veneziani*, in *Opere politiche*, ed. Furio Diaz (Milan: Marzorati, 1974), vol. 1, 181–370 and 27–152; and Antonio Brucioli, *Dialogi*, ed. Aldo Landi (Naples and Chicago: Prismi–The Newberry Library, 1990). An interesting study of Florentine political thought during the transition from the republic of Soderini to the principality of Cosimo I can be found in Rudolf von Albertini, *Firenze dalla repubblica al principato* (Turin: Einaudi, 1970).

In the late seventeenth century the centers of republican political thought shifted to the Netherlands and England. An important text of Dutch republicanism is Pieter de la Court and Johan de Witt, *Interest van Holland* (1642), which was translated into English in 1702 (*The True Interest and Political Maxims of the Republick of Holland and West-Friesland*). It contains a key defense of the principle that republican government is the best suited to the prosperity of a commercial society.

For English republicanism the central work from a historical and theoretical point of view is James Harrington, *The Commonwealth of Oceana; and, A System of Politics* (1656), ed. J. G. A. Pocock (Cambridge, U.K.: Cambridge University Press, 1992). In the preliminaries, Harrington responds to the critique of the ideal of republican liberty that Thomas Hobbes set forth in Chapter 21 of *Leviathan*. Other essential texts are: Henry Neville, *Plato Redivivus, or A Dialogue concerning Government*, and Walter Moyle, *Essay upon the Constitution of the Roman Government*, both in *Two English Republican Tracts*, ed. Caroline

Bibliography

Robbins (Cambridge, U.K.: Cambridge University Press, 1969); Alger-
non Sidney, *Discourses concerning Government*, ed. Thomas G. West
(Indianapolis: Liberty Classics, 1990); and John Milton, *Defence of the
People of England*, in *The Works of John Milton* (New York: Columbia
University Press, 1932), vol. 7, and *The Readie and Easie Way to Estab-
lish a Free Commonwealth*, in *Complete Prose Works of John Milton* (New
Haven, Conn.: Yale University Press, 1980), vol. 7.

For European republican political thought in the eighteenth century,
an indispensable guide is still Franco Venturi, *Utopia and Reform in the
Enlightenment* (Cambridge, U.K.: Cambridge University Press, 1971).
Likewise, it is indispensable to begin with *The Spirit of Laws* (Berkeley:
University of California Press, 1977), even if Montesquieu was no
republican. And the canonical texts are those by Jean-Jacques Rousseau,
especially *The Social Contract and the Discourses* (New York: Everyman's
Library, 1993).

To gain a picture of republican political thought in the revolution-
ary period, one should read the collection titled *Aux origines de la
république, 1789–1792*, with a preface by Maurice Agulhon and introduction by Marcel Dorigny (Paris: EDHIS, 1992), 6 vols., as well as
Maximilien Robespierre. Also from the late eighteenth century is the
essay in which Immanuel Kant states that a republican constitution is
the prerequisite for perpetual peace (*Perpetual Peace and Other Essays on
Politics, History, and Moral Practice*, ed. and trans. Ted Humphrey [Indi-
anapolis: Hackett, 1982]). Among Italian political works of a republican
bent at that time, the writings of Francesco Mario Pagano and Eleonora
Pimentel Fonseca, both of whom were martyrs for the Neapolitan
Republic of 1799, are notable. And of course, for republican political
thought in the United States, the fundamental texts are Thomas Paine,
The Rights of Man, and Alexander Hamilton, John Jay, and James Madi-
son, *The Federalist Papers*.

In the nineteenth century, Italy's most significant republican works
were those of Carlo Cattaneo, especially those in which he discussed his
theory of federalism, and Giuseppi Mazzini. In England the works of
John Stuart Mill abound with fertile republican ideas, notably *Considerations on Representative Government* and *On Liberty*.

Notes

Introduction: A New Interpretation of Republicanism

1. See, for instance, Michael Sandel, *Democracy's Discontent* (Cambridge, Mass.: Harvard University Press, 1998), 5–7; Roger Smith, *Civic Ideals* (New Haven, Conn.: Yale University Press, 1997), 35–37 and 82.

2. *Codex* 5.59.5.

3. Schumpeter's well-known remark—"There is, first, no such thing as a uniquely determined common good that all people could agree on or be made to agree on by the force of rational argument"—is perfectly correct, but it does not apply to the republican conception of the common good I am outlining here. See Joseph A. Schumpeter, *Capitalism, Socialism, and Democracy* (New York: Harper Bros., 1950), 251.

4. See Niccolò Machiavelli, *Discourses on Livy*, trans. Harvey C. Mansfield and Nathan Tarcov (Chicago: University of Chicago Press, 1996), II.2.

5. Francesco Guicciardini, *Dialogue on the Government of Florence* (Cambridge, U.K.: Cambridge University Press, 1994), 99–100.

6. See Donato Giannotti, *Della repubblica fiorentina*, in *Opere politiche*, ed. Furio Diaz (Milan: Marzorati, 1974), vol. 1, 214. See

Notes

also Niccolò Machiavelli, *Sommario delle cose della città di Lucca*, in *Opere politiche*, ed. Corrado Vivanti (Turin: Einaudi-Gallimard, 1997), vol. 1, 718–19.

7. See Machiavelli, *Discourses on Livy*, I.5 and I.58.

8. Jean-Jacques Rousseau, *Lettres écrites de la montagne*, in *Oeuvres complètes* (Paris: Gallimard, 1964), vol. 3, 889.

9. Margaret Canovan, "Patriotism Is Not Enough," *British Journal of Political Science* 30 (2000): 413–32. She refers to my book *For Love of Country* (Oxford: Oxford University Press, 1997).

10. Carlo Pisacane, *La rivoluzione*, in Franco della Peruta, ed., *Scrittori politici dell'Ottocento* (Milan and Naples, n.d.), vol. 1, 1181, 1184.

11. See Amy Gutmann, "Democracy and Its Discontents," in *Liberal Modernism and Democratic Equality: George Kateb and the Practice of Politics*, ed. Austin Sarat and Dana Villa (Princeton, N.J.: Princeton University Press, 1996); see also Amy Gutmann and Dennis Thompson, *Democracy and Disagreement* (Cambridge, Mass.: Belknap Press of Harvard University Press, 1996), and "Democratic Disagreement," in *Deliberative Politics: Essays on Democracy and Disagreement*, ed. Stephen Macedo (Oxford: Oxford University Press, 1999), 243–79.

12. George Kateb, "Is Patriotism a Mistake?" *Social Research* 67 (2000): 901–24.

13. See his *Republicanism: A Theory of Freedom and Government* (Oxford: Oxford University Press, 1999), 185–89. Michael Walzer has nicely described deliberation as "a particular way of thinking: quiet, reflective, open to a wide range of evidence, respectful of different views. It is a rational process of weighing the available data, considering alternative possibilities, arguing about relevance and worthiness, and then choosing the best policy or person." "Deliberation, and What Else?" in *Deliberative Politics*, ed. Macedo, 58.

1. The Story Begins in Italy

1. Useful in this connection is the dispute between Dario Antiseri and Michele Salvati published in *Liberal* 1, no. 7 (1998): 89–93. An admirable exception is Gian Enrico Rusconi, *Patria e repubblica* (Bologna: Mulino, 1997). Rusconi suggests "reviving the spirit of

republicanism, reconjugating liberty and fatherland with a code and language that belong to us and to our time." I fully agree about reactivating the spirit of republicanism, and I believe, as I shall try to demonstrate here, that classical republicanism and Italian humanism are still capable of providing us with the concepts of civic virtue, liberty, and fatherland that can be the fundamental core of a rediscovered republican language.

2. Modern political thinkers have offered harsh condemnations of the Italian republics. In Chapter 21 of *Leviathan*, Hobbes, in a passage that requires no commentary, ridiculed the claims of Lucca and all the republics to be repositories of true political liberty: "There is written on the turrets of the city of Lucca in great characters at this day, the word LIBERTAS; yet no man can thence infer that a particular man has more liberty or immunity from the service of the Commonwealth there than in Constantinople. Whether a Commonwealth be monarchical or popular, the freedom is still the same." Montesquieu, the acknowledged master of constitutionalism, presents the Italian republics as realms of the arbitrary and, as Hobbes had done with Lucca, compares Venice to Constantinople. "In the republics of Italy," he writes in the chapter of *The Spirit of Laws* in which he sets forth his theory of the separation of powers, "where these three powers are united, there is less liberty than in our monarchies. Hence their government is obliged to have recourse to as violent methods for its support as even that of the Turks, witness the state inquisitors and the lion's mouth into which every informer may at all hours throw his written accusations."

Equally harsh was the verdict of Alexander Hamilton in *The Federalist Papers*, one of the fundamental texts of American democracy: "It is impossible to read the history of the petty republics of Greece and Italy without feeling sensations of horror and disgust at the distractions with which they were continually agitated, and at the rapid succession of revolutions by which they were kept in a state of perpetual vibration between the extremes of tyranny and anarchy." *The Federalist Papers* (New York: Modern Library, n.d.), 76.

Whereas for Montesquieu the chief failing of the Italian republics had been that they were unable to institute a true separation of powers, for Hamilton they had proved incapable of curing the ills of factions. The former defect denied them the status of models of liberty; the latter downgraded them to negative examples of permanent instability. If we pass from the liberals to the Marxists, things look no better. Antonio Gramsci considered the free communes an expression of the primitive, economic-corporativist phase of the modern state. With the intellectual courage found only in the great, he wrote about the last Florentine Republic, in 1530: "That Maramaldo could be a representative of historical progress and Ferrucci might be in historical terms a throwback, might prove morally unappetizing, but historically it may and must be upheld." For Gramsci, the free republic belonged to the past, a past from which not even Machiavelli—although he did understand "that only an absolute monarch can resolve the problems of the era"—was able to escape. Gramsci, *Prison Notebooks*, vol. 2, ed. and trans. Joseph A. Buttigieg (New York: Columbia University Press, 1996).

3. Forgotten, that is, by the great majority of Italians but not all. Every year on February 9 republicans, especially in Romagna, solemnly celebrate the anniversary of the Roman Republic of 1849. In 1999, on the occasion of the second centennial of the Neapolitan Republic of 1799, the Italian Institute for Philosophical Studies undertook initiatives of great intellectual and civic value.

4. See the letter of March 4, 1506, from Francesco Cardinal Soderini to Machiavelli, cited in Niccolò Machiavelli, *Opere*, ed. Franco Gaeta (Turin: UTET, 1984), vol. 3, 217.

5. Donato Giannotti, *Della repubblica fiorentina*, in *Opere politiche*, ed. Furio Diaz (Milan: Marzorati, 1974), vol. 1, 240–41. See also Marino Berengo, *Nobili e mercanti nella Lucca del Cinquecento* (Turin: Einaudi, 1965), 31.

6. See Nicolai Rubinstein, "Machiavelli and the Florentine Republican Experience," in *Machiavelli and Republicanism*, ed. Gisela Bock, Quentin Skinner, and Maurizio Viroli (Cambridge, U.K.: Cambridge University Press, 1990), 9–15.

7. Mario Ascheri, "La Siena del 'Buon Governo' (1287–1355)," in *Politica e cultura nelle repubbliche italiane dal Medioevo all'età moderna: Firenze, Genova, Lucca, Siena, Venezia*, ed. Mario Ascheri and S. Adorni Braccesi (Rome: Istituto Storico Italiano per l'Età Moderna e Contemporanea, 2001).

8. R. Ferrante, "Legge e repubblica: L'esperienza genovese fra XIV e XVI secolo," in *Politica e cultura*, ed. Ascheri and Braccesi.

9. Simonde de Sismondi, *Storia delle repubbliche italiane*, ed. Pierangelo Schiera (Turin: Bollati Boringhieri, 1996), 5.

10. Carlo Cattaneo, "La città considerata come principio ideale delle istorie italiane," in *Opere scelte*, ed. Delia Castelnuovo Frigessi (Turin: Einaudi, 1972), vol. 4, 123.

11. See Robert Putnam, *Making Democracy Work* (Princeton, N.J.: Princeton University Press, 1993).

12. See "Laudatio Florentinae Urbis," in *From Petrarch to Leonardo Bruni*, ed. Hans Baron (Chicago: University of Chicago Press, 1968), 260; the source is *Corpus iuris civilis, Codex* 5.59.5.2: "Quod omnes similiter tangit, ab omnibus comprobetur."

13. Francesco Guicciardini, *Considerazioni intorno ai "Discorsi" del Machiavelli*, in Niccolò Machiavelli, *Discorsi sopra la prima deca di Tito Livio*, ed. Corrado Vivanti (Turin: Einaudi, 1983), 526.

14. Giannotti, *Della repubblica fiorentina*, 214.

15. Niccolò Machiavelli, *Istorie fiorentine*, IV.1; see *Opere*, ed. Alessandro Montevecchi, vol. 2, 468–69.

16. Niccolò Machiavelli, *Sommario delle cose della città di Lucca*, in *Opere politiche*, ed. Corrado Vivanti (Turin: Einaudi-Gallimard, 1997), vol. 1, 718–19.

17. In an important essay Elena Fasano Guarini has reconstructed the complex and fascinating history of the survival of republican political values among Florentine exiles in the sixteenth century. This was, she writes, a world of "dispersion and often drift, subject to the opposing temptations of return and a new integration into the countries in which one found hospitality." But she also cautions that the history of sixteenth-century Italian republicanism cannot be reduced merely to the story of the exiled and politically defeated Florentines or to the "cautious and tacit dissent that insinuated itself even in Florence, within an official mouthpiece of the principality, such as the Accademia Fiorentina." Historians should also look to the "more 'silent' republics, which survived longer, the depictions that they offered of themselves, the ways in which that image was received, the republican language that thus developed and

its assonances and dissonances with the Florentine republic." See her "Declino e durata delle repubbliche e delle idee repubblicane nell'Italia del Cinquecento," in *Libertà politica e virtù civile*, ed. Maurizio Viroli (forthcoming).

18. Even among scholars of the history of political thought, the idea is widespread that republicanism survived in the age of monarchies as an archaic critique of the present. See J. G. A. Pocock, "La repubblica come critica del mutamento storico," in *Libertà politica e virtù civile*, ed. Viroli.

19. Franco Venturi, *Utopia and Reform in the Enlightenment* (Cambridge, U.K.: Cambridge University Press, 1971), 71.

20. See K. Backer, "Le trasformazioni del repubblicanesimo classico nella Francia del Settecento," in *Libertà politica e virtù civile*, ed. Viroli.

21. Machiavelli, *Discourses on Livy*, I.45.

22. The equality for which "brave and earnest British women" were struggling, wrote Mazzini, must be considered "sacred for any sensible, logical, and fearless man who fights for any question involving Equality, to whatever class or section of mankind it applies" (letter to Emilia Venturi, May 2, 1870, in *Scritti editi e inediti di Giuseppe Mazzini* [Imola: Paolo Gallati, 1906], vol. 89, 152–59). To an American correspondent who asked his advice on the question of voting rights for blacks in the United States he replied: "You have abolished slavery. This abolition is the crown of your glorious strife, the religious consequence of your battles, which otherwise would only have been a lamentable butchery. You have decreed that the sun of the Republic shall shine freely upon all; that as God is one, so on the blessed soil where liberty is not merely a chance fact but a faith and a gospel, the stamp of Humanity shall be one. Can you mutilate this great principle? Can you curtail and reduce it to the proportions of the semi-liberty of the monarchies? Can you tolerate that any man among you should be only half of himself? Can you proclaim the dogma of semi-responsibility? Can you constitute on the republican soil of America a class of political slaves like those of the Middle Ages? Does liberty exist without the vote?" (letter to Conway, October 30, 1865, in *Scritti editi e inediti*, vol. 88, 163–64).

23. Carlo Cattaneo, *Stati uniti d'Italia*, ed. Norberto Bobbio (Turin:

Chiantore, 1945), 34–35 and 149. Bobbio thought that Cattaneo was "liberal and federalist by conviction, and therefore in essence," and "republican by reaction, and thus by accident" (32), that he derived his federalism from liberalism and was especially influenced by Benjamin Constant, Sismondi, and Tocqueville. But Cattaneo's federal republic, for which the United States and Switzerland served as models, was a development of republican, not liberal, political thought. Suffice it to quote *The Federalist Papers*: "In the extent and proper structure of the Union, therefore, we behold a republican remedy for the diseases most incident to republican government. And according to the degree of pleasure and pride we feel in being republicans, ought to be our zeal in cherishing the spirit and supporting the character of Federalists" (62). To which we should add that Tocqueville described as the "reflective patriotism of a republic" that civic sense which Cattaneo praised as the finest fruit of municipal self-rule.

24. Carlo Cattaneo, *Scritti politici ed epistolario*, ed. Gabriele Rosa and Jesse White Mario (Florence: Barbera, 1894), vol. 1, 263.

2. The New Utopia of Liberty

1. See Philip Pettit, *Republicanism: A Theory of Freedom and Government*, 2nd ed. (Oxford: Oxford University Press, 1998).

2. Francesco Mario Pagano, *La coscienza della libertà: Dai "Saggi politici" al progetto di Costituzione*, ed. Renato Bruschi (Naples: Generoso Procaccini, 1998), 73.

3. Montesquieu, *The Spirit of Laws* (Berkeley: University of California Press, 1977), XI.6.

4. Jean-Jacques Rousseau, *Des lois*, in *Oeuvres complètes*, ed. Bernard Gagnebin and Marcel Raymond (Paris: Gallimard, 1964), vol. 3, 492.

5. Benjamin Constant, "The Liberty of the Ancients Compared with That of the Moderns," in *Political Writings* (Cambridge, U.K.: Cambridge University Press, 1999), 310–11. Isaiah Berlin, "Two Concepts of Liberty," in *The Proper Study of Mankind*, ed. Henry Hardy (New York: Farrar, Straus and Giroux, 1998).

6. Norberto Bobbio, *Politica e cultura* (1955; Turin: Einaudi, 1974), 172–74.

3. *The Value of Republican Liberty*

1. See Quentin Skinner, "Machiavelli and the Maintenance of Liberty," *Politics* 18 (1983): 3–15; "The Idea of Negative Liberty: Philosophical and Historical Perspectives," in *Philosophy in History*, ed. Richard Rorty, J. B. Schneewind, and Quentin Skinner (Cambridge, U.K.: Cambridge University Press, 1984), 193–221; "The Paradoxes of Political Liberty," in *The Tanner Lectures on Human Values*, vol. 7, ed. Sterling M. McMurrin (Salt Lake City: University of Utah Press, 1986), 225–50; and *Liberty before Liberalism* (Cambridge, U.K.: Cambridge University Press, 1998), 84, n. 55.

2. "Republicanism: Once More with Hindsight," afterword to the second edition of Philip Pettit, *Republicanism: A Theory of Freedom and Government* (Oxford: Oxford University Press, 1998).

3. Skinner, *Liberty before Liberalism*, 84.

4. Isaiah Berlin, "Two Concepts of Liberty," in *The Proper Study of Mankind*, ed. Henry Hardy (New York: Farrar, Straus and Giroux, 1998), 148.

5. "Liberi iam hinc populi Romani res pace belloque gestas, annuos magistratus, imperiaque legum potentiora quam hominum peragam," Livy, *Ab urbe condita*, II.I.1. "Nam quid a Pyrro, Hannibale, Philippoque et Antiocho defensum est aliud quam libertas et suae cuique sedes, neu cui nisi legibus pareremus?" Sallust, *Orationes et epistulae excertae de historiis*, 4, Loeb Classical Library. Cicero, *Pro Cluentio*, trans. H. Grose Hodge (1927; Cambridge, Mass.: Harvard University Press, 1990), IX.146.

6. Coluccio Salutati to Niccolodio Bartolomei, April 1369, in *Epistolario di Coluccio Salutati*, ed. Francesco Novati (Rome: Forzani, 1891–1911), vol. 1, 90. On Bruni, see Nicolai Rubinstein, "Florentine Constitutionalism and Medici Ascendancy in the Fifteenth Century," in *Florentine Studies*, ed. Nicolai Rubinstein (London: Faber, 1968), 442–61, especially 445; and Leonardo Bruni, *Historiarum Florentini populi libri XII*, ed. Emilio Santini, *Rerum Italicarum Scriptores*, vol. 19, pt. 3 (Bologna, 1914), 82; see also "Laudatio Florentinae Urbis," in *From Petrarch to Leonardo Bruni*, ed. Hans Baron (Chicago: University of Chicago Press, 1968), 259. On Rinuccini, see *Ricordi storici di Filippo di Cino Rinuccini dal*

1282 al 1460 colla continuazione di Alamanno e Neri suoi figli, ed. Giuseppe Aiazzi (Florence: Piatti, 1840), 103.

7. Machiavelli, *Discourses*, I.5.29; foreword to *Florentine Histories*, IV.

8. See Livy, II.15.3.

9. Machiavelli, *Discourses*, II.2.

10. Ibid., I.37.

11. James Harrington, *The Commonwealth of Oceana, and A System of Politics*, ed. J. G. A. Pocock (Cambridge, U.K.: Cambridge University Press, 1992), 20.

12. John Locke, *An Essay concerning the True Original, Extent, and End of Civil Government*, 57.29, in *Two Treatises of Government*, ed. Peter Laslett (Cambridge, U.K.: Cambridge University Press, 1998).

13. See Skinner, *Liberty before Liberalism*, 84.

14. See Norberto Bobbio, "Della libertà dei moderni comparata a quella dei posteri," in *Politica e cultura* (1955; Turin: Einaudi, 1974), 160–94.

15. Ann Phillips, "Feminism and Republicanism: Is This a Plausible Alliance?," speech delivered at a conference titled "The Historical Perspectives of Republicanism and the Future of the European Union," Siena, September 24–27, 1998.

4. Republicanism, Liberalism, and Communitarianism

1. See Norberto Bobbio, *Politica e cultura* (1955; Turin: Einaudi, 1974), 269–82.

2. Machiavelli, *Discourses*, I.25 and I.58.

3. "Hanc enim ob causam maxime, ut sua tenerentur, res publicae civitatesque constitutae sunt."

4. Machiavelli, *Discourses*, I.16.

5. Ibid., I.4.

6. See Roger Boesche, "Thinking about Freedom," *Political Theory* 26 (1998): 863.

7. Stephen Holmes, *Passions and Constraint: On the Theory of Liberal Democracy* (Chicago: University of Chicago Press, 1995).

8. Alexis de Tocqueville, *Democracy in America*, ed. J. P. Mayer, trans. George Lawrence (New York: Harper & Row, 1969), 237–40.

9. Jürgen Habermas, *Faktizität und Geltung* (Frankfurt: Suhrkamp, 1992), 640; and *Die Nachholende Revolution* (Frankfurt: Suhrkamp, 1990), 208.

10. See, for instance, Don Herzog, "Some Questions for Republicans," *Political Theory* 14 (1986): 486, and Charles Taylor, "Cross-Purposes: The Liberal-Communitarian Debate," in *Liberalism and the Moral Life*, ed. Nancy L. Rosenblum (Cambridge, Mass.: Harvard University Press, 1989), 165 and 177; Michael Sandel, *Democracy's Discontent* (Cambridge, Mass.: Harvard University Press, 1998); Michael Walzer, "Rescuing Civil Society," *Dissent* (Winter 1999): 62–67; David Miller, introduction to *Liberty*, ed. David Miller (Oxford: Oxford University Press, 1991), 6; David Wootton, "Introduction: The Republican Tradition: From Commonwealth to Common Sense," 17–18, and Blair Worden, "Republicanism and the Restoration, 1660–1683," 174, in *Republicanism, Liberty, and Commercial Society, 1649–1776*, ed. David Wootton (Stanford, Calif.: Stanford University Press, 1994).

11. In reference to public and private charity, the words of Mazzini still apply: "Christian charity was a means to improve one's soul rather than a consciousness about a common goal to be obtained, by the will of God, here on earth: it never went beyond the limits of almsgiving or philanthropy; where the adherents to the new religion found the hungry, they fed them, they dressed the naked, they surrounded the sick with care; but there was never a thought to how to remove the reasons for poverty and nakedness." "Dal Concilio a Dio," in *Scritti editi e inediti di Giuseppe Mazzini* (Imola: Paolo Gallati, 1906), vol. 86, 241 ff.

5. Republican Virtue

1. See in this connection Michael Walzer, *What It Means to Be an American* (New York: Marsilio, 1992), 81–101.

2. See Montesquieu, *The Spirit of Laws* (Berkeley: University of California Press, 1977), IV.5.

3. Ibid., VIII.16.

4. *Epistolario di Coluccio Salutati*, ed. Francesco Novati (Rome: Forzani, 1891–1911), vol. 1, 197–98.

5. Matteo Palmieri, *Vita civile*, ed. Gino Belloni (Florence: Olschki, 1981), 7 and 54.

6. Leon Battista Alberti, *The Family in Renaissance Florence*, trans. R. N. Watkins (Columbia: University of South Carolina Press, 1969).

7. Cited in Hans Baron, *In Search of Florentine Civic Humanism* (Princeton, N.J.: Princeton University Press, 1988), vol. 2, 229–50.

8. Palmieri, *Vita civile*, 63 and 151.

9. Machiavelli, *Discourses*, I.16.

10. Ibid., II.2.

11. Ibid., I.10.

12. Ibid., I.37.

13. Alexis de Tocqueville, *Democracy in America*, 94–95.

6. Republican Patriotism

1. Machiavelli, *Discourses*, II.2.

2. Rosario Villari, "Patriottismo e riforma politica," in *Libertà politica e virtù civile*, ed. Maurizio Viroli (forthcoming).

3. *Encyclopédie* (Neuchâtel: Bouloiseau, 1765), vol. 12, 178 and 180.

4. Jean-Jacques Rousseau, *Economie politique*, in *Oeuvres complètes*, ed. Bernard Gagnebin and Marcel Raymond (Paris: Gallimard, 1964), vol. 3, 258.

5. Concerning the difference between *patrie* and *pays*, see *Emile*, in *Oeuvres complètes*, vol. 4, 858, where Rousseau writes, "Those who have no homeland at least have a country," and *La Nouvelle Héloïse*, in *Ouevres complètes*, vol. 2, 657: "The more closely I consider this little State, the more I think that it is a fine thing to have a homeland, and may the Lord preserve from harm all those who believe that they have a homeland [*patrie*], and in fact have nothing more than a country [*pays*]!"

6. Rousseau to Lieutenant Colonel Charles Pictet, in *Correspondance complète de Jean-Jacques Rousseau*, ed. R. A. Leigh, 53 vols. (Geneva: Droz, 1965–1995), vol. 19, 190.

7. Gaetano Filangieri, *La scienza della legislazione*, ed. Renato Bruschi (Naples: Generoso Procaccini, 1995), IV, pt. 2a, 42.

Notes

8. Giandomenico Romagnosi, "Istituzioni di civile filosofia," in *Opere*, ed. Alessandro de Giorgi (Milan: Perelli and Mariani, later Volpato, 1841–1848), vol. 3, 1548.

9. Alexis de Tocqueville, *Democracy in America*, 68.

10. Carlo Cattaneo, *Sulla legge comunale e provinciale*, in *Opere scelte*, ed. Delia Castelnuovo Frigessi (Turin: Einaudi, 1972), vol. 4, 406.

11. Giuseppe Mazzini, *Scritti politici*, ed. Terenzio Grandi and Augusto Comba (Turin: UTET, 1972), 885.

12. Ibid., 882 and 872.

13. Ibid., 882.

14. See Quintilian, *Institutio oratoria*, V.10.24–25, and Cicero, *De officiis*, I.17.53.

15. Antonio Brucioli, *Dialogi*, ed. Aldo Landi (Naples and Chicago: Prismi–The Newberry Library, 1990), 112.

16. John Stuart Mill, *A System of Logic, Ratiocinative and Inductive* (1843), VI.10.5.

17. M. L. Salvadori, "La tradizione repubblicana nell'Italia dell'800 e del 900," in *Libertà politica e virtù civile*, ed. Viroli.

18. Giacomo Ulivi, in *Lettere della Resistenza europea*, ed. Giovanni Pirelli (Turin: Einaudi, 1969), 229.

19. Machiavelli, *Discourses*, II.2 and I.11.

20. See Tocqueville, *Democracy in America*, 290–301 and 444.

21. Ibid., 94.

22. Norberto Bobbio, "Politica laica," in *Tra due repubbliche* (Rome: Donzelli, 1996), 37.

23. Machiavelli, *Discourses*, III.1.

24. See Martha Minow, *Between Vengeance and Forgiveness: Facing History after Genocide and Mass Violence* (Boston: Beacon Press, 1998), 11 ff.

Index

Index

Index